Parenting First Aid

Hope for the Discouraged
Study Guide

MARTY MACHOWSKI

New
Growth
Press

newgrowthpress.com

New Growth Press, Greensboro, NC 27404
www.newgrowthpress.com
Copyright © 2020 by Marty Machowski

Cover Design: Faceout Books, faceoutstudio.com
Interior Design and Typesetting: Gretchen Logterman

ISBN: 978-1-64507-046-7 (Print)
ISBN: 978-1-64507-047-4 (eBook)

Printed in India

27 26 25 24 23 22 21 20   1 2 3 4 5

Contents

LEADER'S NOTES

First Aid for Parents

All parents go through seasons of trial, and yet not everyone has a context to share their struggles and join with others in prayer. Parents think they are alone in their trials and do their best to bear up under their challenges. The result is that we have churches full of parents who feel they are the only family with struggles. Though parents have a desire to open up, it's hard to be the first one to share. *Parenting First Aid* and this accompanying study guide are designed to help parents get that conversation started. To make that a little easier, I've included many of my own family's struggles within these pages. Hopefully, that will help break the ice for others to share.

Your task as a leader is to foster the kind of small group discussion environment where people feel safe but not pressured to share their struggles. The best way to create a safe zone for sharing is by your example. When a leader shares their challenges and failures, it helps others feel more comfortable doing the same. It is only after we open up and share our challenges that people can comfort us in our trials with the comfort they themselves have received from God (2 Corinthians 1:4).

Parents often don't know who to ask for help or don't have relationships with other parents that are deep enough to overcome their reluctance to share. Pulling parents together for a study like this provides the ramp up for those parents and gives them the opportunity to benefit from the insights and biblical wisdom of the other participants in your group.

As long we keep our challenges to ourselves, folks won't know to pray for us. It is my desire that, with honest sharing about our struggles, those who are going through seasons of parenting trial will discover God's grace and those who are walking in a season of blessing will be better prepared for the seasons of trial that are sure to come.

Some folks will share their struggles quickly while others may take weeks to open up. Your job is to foster an environment where people are comfortable and can share as much or as little as they like. It is also important to remember that some details are too sensitive to share with a group, and yet a lot can be communicated without disclosing the specifics of a situation. The important thing is that we all drop the façade of trial-free parenting and join in to pray for and encourage one another as we walk through one of the greatest challenges we face in life.

Stressing the importance of confidentiality and offering regular reminders will help folks who want to share but feel unsure. This will also encourage those who may be gossip-prone to protect their fellow group participants by maintaining strict confidentiality.

How the Study Works

Timeframe

Parenting First Aid, the companion book to this study, is designed as a devotional that you walk through slowly rather than just read cover to cover. So allow for time between small group meetings. Rather than meeting ten weeks in a row to complete the material, plan to allow at least two weeks between discussions. The discussions each cover two chapters from *Parenting First Aid*, so this will allow participants to read and review one chapter of *Parenting First Aid* per week. There are ten discussions in this study guide. This means you should plan on at least twenty weeks to finish the study, since you have two weeks between discussions.

Preparation

Each discussion has two main parts: preparation and the study session. Participants should prepare for each meeting by completing the preparation part beforehand. It will tell them which chapters in *Parenting First Aid* to read each week, give them a brief review of that material, and ask them to reflect on three to five questions. The questions are designed to help them digest the material they read and begin to apply it to their lives. Encourage them to write down their answers. This will help them recall their thoughts later when the study group meets.

The Study

When you meet, plan to spend some warm-up social time before and after your discussion. If you set aside two hours for your meeting, you can allow for a half hour up front and again after the study. This time is important to allow participants to get to know each other, and it also gives them time after the study to ask questions privately of one another. One important purpose of any study is to foster relationships that will carry on long after the formal meetings have ended.

Begin your discussion by reviewing the previous lesson's action steps, and by going over some of the written answers that were part of everyone's preparation. There are more preparation questions for each chapter of *Parenting First Aid* than you will be able to cover during your discussion time. The primary benefit to the participants comes from having answered the questions, not discussing them. So encourage folks to answer their written questions honestly, for their own benefit, even if they are not comfortable sharing once the group meets. Pick and choose questions for discussion that you think will best serve your group. Having many questions makes it easier for you to ask folks to pick one answer to share with the group. Even the most reluctant person can usually find one question they are comfortable talking about.

Next, the **Refuel** section introduces a Bible passage on prayer not found in *Parenting First Aid*. The goal of this section is to regularly remind folks in your study of the importance of prayer. You should discuss at least one of the questions from this section each week of your study to help your parents maintain a healthy prayer life. There is no more important goal of this study than to connect parents to our God who reigns over their family.

The **Relate** section provides a portion of a chapter from *Parenting First Aid* that you can read together during your study. This lets someone who has fallen behind in their reading still benefit from part of the book and discuss it. You can read the excerpt yourself, invite someone to read it, or go around the room and have each person read a paragraph.

If you choose the latter, be aware that not everyone feels comfortable reading out loud in a group. So know your participants and ask folks ahead of time to let you know if they are uncomfortable reading out loud. If you are unsure, simply ask for volunteers to read aloud.

The **Respond** section is a time for group prayer, and also gives participants a few action steps to complete during the coming week to help put what they are learning into practice. Then, each lesson ends with a Scripture to memorize in the **Remember** section. Encourage folks to memorize each of the verses listed and give opportunity during your time together to test them. Most people can remember these verses with a little encouragement and accountability. Invite participants to write out an index card for each of the verses with the reference on one side and the Scripture on the other. People will say they "can't memorize," but that is only because they have never tried seriously or took on too great a memorization task. Encourage everyone to give it a try and set as a minimum goal to memorize at least half the listed verses.

Discussion Guidelines

Never call on a participant to share unless you've asked them if they are comfortable sharing. Instead, invite folks to contribute more generally with questions like, "Who would like to share their answer to one of the questions in this section?" or, "Who would like to share how well the action steps from the past few studies have served them?" Set up a pattern of moving on to the next question before everyone has had a chance to answer. That will keep folks interested and remove an awkward moment if one or more persons are uncomfortable answering a particular question. At other times, with more general questions, you can ask everyone to answer.

Not everyone in your group will be struggling with major parenting challenges. You may have new parents with young children whose biggest trial is getting their two-year-old to stay in bed in the evening. They may feel their struggle is too trivial to introduce to the group. Be sure to invite parents with younger children to share some of the challenges they are facing or share their fears and anxieties regarding a particular situation. On the other hand, one of your participants may be going through an exceptionally difficult trial as compared to the others in your group. Be sensitive to their needs.

As the leader, if you are willing to open up your life and struggles and become vulnerable to the group, it will help create a safe atmosphere for sharing. It can also help to encourage a seasoned parent who has walked through trials to open up the sharing time with a testimony of some of the trials they've walked through. Christians thrive in an atmosphere of honest disclosure, but this requires the utmost of confidentiality. So remind your folks often that the discussions in the group are confidential.

Any time you draw together a group of parents who are sharing about their parenting challenges you must be prepared for how to handle a disclosure of abuse. It can be helpful at the outset to communicate with the group that while strict confidentiality must be maintained, the exception to that is when the life of a child is in danger or a report of child sexual abuse must be made to the proper authorities. If you explain this at the very start of the study, it will help position you to make a report should a participant reveal their child has been abused. Know your state's reporting laws ahead of leading your discussion group.

Measuring Success

One goal of a small group study is to help folks read the material and relate it to their lives. Consider it a huge success even if a person gets through the study without sharing once publicly, but they complete the questions and engage the book. The vast majority of people who purchase a book never open it or only read the first chapter before the busyness of life draws them away. Any extent that people open up and engage in biblical fellowship over their struggles is icing on the cake.

As your study ends, encourage folks to stay connected and continue praying for one another. Remind them that every book we read becomes a tool for us to use to encourage others. They will undoubtedly run into other parents who are walking through trials and could benefit from *Parenting First Aid*. Close out your time reminding folks of the importance of maintaining confidentiality.

May God bless your study through *Parenting First Aid* and encourage you with the truth that God is with you and his grace is sufficient.

A FAITH-FILLED PARENT

Main Idea

When we are tempted to give up, we can draw strength from knowing God rules over our lives and families and has not forgotten us.

To Prepare for Your Study Session

WEEK ONE

Read

This study guide and *Parenting First Aid* are designed to give you two weeks to prepare for each study session. Over the course of your first week, reflect on Psalm 139 by reading chapter 1 in *Parenting First Aid*.

Review

Life as a parent runs pretty smoothly during those seasons when our plans fall into place and things go well. But when our days don't go according to plan and those days turn into weeks, we can experience anxiety and fear. When we walk through these seasons of trial, we can be tempted to think things are running out of control. While our situation may get beyond our ability to control, it is never beyond God's control. Psalm 139 reassures us that God knows all and controls all, and that nothing happens beyond his rule and his reign.

Reflect

As you read through chapter 1 in *Parenting First Aid*, or when you finish, answer the following questions. Writing down your responses will help you think carefully and remember them. You'll have a chance to share some of your answers, if you want, when your study session meets.

1. Which truth in Psalm 139:1–12 is hardest for you to believe: that God is all present, that he knows your situation, or that he cares for you? Why?

2. What is most encouraging to you in this psalm?

3. How can you find comfort in knowing that God planned every one of your days and they are written in his book?

4. How have you seen God use the trials of your life for your good? How have they shaped you?

WEEK TWO

Read

During your second week of preparation for the study session, read through chapter 2 of *Parenting First Aid*. It will help you think through Galatians 6:7–10.

Review

We become weary when our parenting challenges linger and don't resolve. We tire at the end of a long day of physical labor, but weariness is more than physical exhaustion; weariness is tiredness of soul. A good night's rest will cure an aching body, but weariness requires an added injection of faith. If left unchecked, our weariness can lead us to lose all faith for change and give up. Paul speaks to this condition in Galatians 6 and encourages the Galatians by reminding them of the harvest which comes to the person who refuses to give in to weariness or give up on God.

Reflect

Answer these questions as you read through *Parenting First Aid* chapter 2. You will have an opportunity to share some of your responses when the study session meets.

5. Where are you most tempted to give up because you haven't seen good fruit for your efforts or prayers?

6. Why do you hesitate to share your struggles with others? What excuses do you typically make for keeping your challenges to yourself?

7. Who are the people God wants you to share your trials with and ask for advice and prayer? Why are they a good choice?

Study Session

Spend the first part of your study going back over the reflection questions you answered during the past few weeks. Pick some of them to discuss, or let each participant share the answers that were most meaningful to them. Then continue with the rest of this study.

Refuel

The Psalms give us a wonderful window into the lives of the men who wrote them. We see their struggles and distress captured in the choice of their words. More importantly, we can see how men like King David trusted God through great difficulty and how they shared their struggles honestly with God. In the following example from Psalm 5, notice how David describes his trial, and be encouraged by his faith that God hears his prayers.

> Give ear to my words, O Lord;
>> consider my groaning.
> Give attention to the sound of my cry,
>> my King and my God,
>> for to you do I pray.
> O Lord, in the morning you hear my voice;
>> in the morning I prepare a sacrifice for you and watch.
> (Psalm 5:1–3)

8. On a scale of 1 to 10 (10 indicating strong faith), how would you rate your trust that God hears your prayers and will answer them for your good? Explain the reasons for your rating.

9. How often do you share the struggles of your heart with God when you pray? Pick the answer below that's most true of you, and explain.

- "Always. I know God loves to listen and help."
- "Often. I'm desperate."
- "Whenever I think of it, but asking God for help doesn't always occur to me."
- "Sometimes, but my first instinct is to try to fix things on my own."
- "Only when I feel a particularly big need."
- "Occasionally, but admitting struggles isn't easy for me."
- "Rarely. I hate to pray and then be disappointed."
- "Hardly ever. Prayer just isn't a big part of my life."
- Other (explain)

10. How could sharing more honestly with God in your prayers help comfort you in your trials?

Relate

Oma's story helped put my parenting trials into perspective. I've never had to start over with nothing. I can't begin to think what it would be like if I lost everything and had to start from scratch. *If God could help them*, I thought, when I first heard this story, *then surely God can help me through my present trials.* Read the story (reprinted from page 27 of *Parenting First Aid*) together, and then discuss the questions that follow.

Oma Petz (*Oma* means "grandmother" in German) was eighty years old when she told my wife and me this story from her childhood. She still remembered the terrifying moments and her uncle's frantic plea as though it happened yesterday. Heinrich Petz lived with his wife, Ida, and their family in a farmhouse he built for them by hand. Late one evening, the entire household, including the young Jewish girl who was staying with them, was awakened from a deep sleep by an uncle's heavy pounding on their front door.

"He told us, 'Move quickly; you must leave now. Take only what you can carry.' We grabbed what we could and climbed into his wagon, not knowing where we were going." The Second World War had finally intruded upon their lives.

When it was safe, Oma's family, along with their young Jewish boarder, returned to their farm to discover a pile of rubble where their stone farmhouse once stood. Shocked by their enormous loss, Heinrich gathered the family to encourage their flagging faith, "We may have lost everything, but we have not lost Jesus," he said. Then he led them in a prayer, thanking God for protecting them and asking the Lord for help and provision. With no place to go, the family slept among the stones that once made up their home.

A few days later, their Jewish houseguest spotted the silhouette of a man rounding a distant hill and immediately recognized his gait. "Papa!" she shouted, and ran to his arms. After hearing how the family had cared for his daughter, the wealthy businessman's heart swelled with thanks. He said to

Heinrich, "I will rebuild your home." He smiled, adding, "On one condition, that you allow my daughter to continue living with you." God had answered their prayer in a matter of days.

The Petz family rebuilt their home, but soon they were once again forced to leave the farmhouse. This time they were displaced by German troops seeking to billet there. Weeks later, when the soldiers left, the family was allowed to reclaim their property. Supplies were gone and the house left a mess, but nothing a week's work couldn't remedy. Later, they were forced out of their home a third and final time and bounced from farm to farm. Most families treated them kindly, but some did no more than toss them a few potatoes.

When WWII ended, they were left homeless because their property was taken from them. Once again Oma remembered her father gathering the family close with the same message: "We may have lost everything, but we have not lost Jesus." Destitute, Heinrich and Ida sent out letters to every distant friend and relation, some in the United States, asking for help.

That was when my wife's grandfather, Carl Rausch, got involved. Concerned about German Christians left destitute after the war, he sponsored them to come to the United States. Carl employed the men in his machine shop in New Haven, Connecticut, and welcomed the Petz family into his own home.

I left our time with Oma grateful for Carl's generosity but even more amazed by Heinrich's faith. Heinrich himself never made it out of Germany, but the prayer he offered in their darkest hour, "We may have lost everything, but we have not lost Jesus," was forever etched upon Oma's heart. Despite losing everything several times over, Heinrich never gave up. He trusted Jesus through it all and in his due season he reaped a wonderful harvest—children, grandchildren, great-grandchildren, and even great-great-grandchildren who love the Lord.

11. How does Heinrich's faith-filled response to his trial, "we may have lost everything, but we have not lost Jesus," build your faith to want to trust God for your life?

12. How can the members of your group be praying for you?

Respond

Take time now for group prayer. Pray for one participant's situation, and for other items springing from this week's study.

Before you leave, plan to take one or more of these *action steps* during the coming week. At the next study session, you'll have a chance to report on how it went.

- Reread Psalm 139:1–12 aloud as your prayer to God. As you read each phrase, make it your own and purpose to believe it in your heart.

- Where do you find yourself struggling most with feeling condemnation as a parent? Make a list of these areas. As you do, remember that as God is at work shaping your children; he is also at work shaping your heart through parenting. Reflect on the gospel, that Jesus died on the cross for all of our sins and failures, taking the punishment we deserve. Then tear up your list, confessing your failures to God and asking for his cleansing forgiveness to wash away your sin.

- Think of three parents you could seek to encourage. (One sure way is to take a week to pray for them and then send an encouraging note to let them know that you did. Mention specific prayers so that your encouragement will sink deeply into their souls.)

Remember

Memorize Galatians 6:9. "And let us not grow weary of doing good, for in due season we will reap, if we do not give up."

A TRUSTING PARENT

Main Idea

Parenting in our own strength only leads to worry.
We need God's help.

To Prepare for Your Study Session

WEEK ONE

Read

During the first week before your study session meets, study Matthew 6:25–34 by working through chapter 3 of *Parenting First Aid*.

Review

Jesus addressed the worry that life can bring when he said, "Do not be anxious about tomorrow, for tomorrow will be anxious for itself" (Matthew 6:34). While his encouragement sounds good, it's not easy to let go of our parenting worries and fears. Often all it takes is to think of all the time our children spend away from us—and worry sets in. *What if they get into trouble? What if they make a bad choice?* Jesus speaks to our worries and fears. He asked, "Why are you anxious about clothing? Consider the lilies of the field, how they grow: they neither toil nor spin, yet I tell you, even Solomon in all his glory was not arrayed like one of these. But if God so clothes the grass of the field, which today is alive and tomorrow is thrown into the oven, will he not much more clothe you, O you of little faith?" (Matthew 6:28–30).

Jesus offers us his promise that if we seek first his kingdom and righteousness he will take care of us. If we put our faith in his promise, we can find rest in the midst of life's greatest challenges, for God always keeps his promises.

Reflect

Answer the following questions as you read through chapter 3 in *Parenting First Aid*, or when you finish. Write your answers down to help you remember them for the study session, when you'll have a chance to discuss them with your group. You'll only share with others what you choose to share, so as you write, be honest with yourself and God.

1. Where are you most prone to worry when it comes to your family? Is it for your material provision, or do you worry about the health, welfare, or the souls of your children?

2. Where do you struggle to trust what God can or will do in your situation? What does it look like to repent of unbelief and start trusting God again?

3. What does it look like to "seek first the kingdom and his righteousness" (Matthew 6:33) for a parent who worries? Think of a specific parenting worry in your life and describe how you might seek God's kingdom first in that situation.

WEEK TWO

Read

Read through chapter 4 of *Parenting First Aid* during your second week of preparation for the study session. It will help you think through Psalm 127.

Review

Every parent learns sooner or later that they can't raise their children without God's help. We must learn to trust and depend on the Spirit of God to do what we can't. We can teach our children to eat, dress themselves, and eventually drive a car, but none of us is able to change a child's heart. Solomon summed up our parenting partnership in Psalm 127 with the opening verse, "Unless the LORD builds the house, those who build it labor in vain." It often takes a trial or difficulty to help us see our need for God. One thing we learn is that the parenting process isn't only producing and maturing a child; God uses parenting to grow and mature us as well.

Reflect

Answer these questions as you read through *Parenting First Aid* chapter 4. Be ready to share some of your responses, if you want, when your study session meets.

4. Reflect on your parenting. In what ways have you been trying to parent alone, apart from God? Try to give a specific example.

5. Where do you most struggle to trust God for your children?

6. How has God taught you to depend on him through the struggles you've endured?

Study Session

Begin this session by reviewing the action steps from the end of the last study. Which steps did you take? What did you learn, or how were you encouraged?

Now go through the reflection questions for this study that you answered during the past few weeks. Pick some of them to discuss, or let each participant share the answers that were most meaningful to them. Then continue with the rest of this study.

Refuel

When Solomon completed the construction of the temple, God gave him a promise that is recorded in 2 Chronicles for us as well. Imagine Solomon having just finished all he set out to accomplish. When times are good, it can feel as though there is little need to call out to God for help. But the Lord knew times of trial would come to Solomon, and gave him a bit of wisdom regarding prayer that serves all of us to remember. The bottom line: God hears the prayers of his children when they turn from their sin and call out to him. Solomon would one day need the words God spoke to him. Instead of continuing to trust the Lord, Solomon later trusted the works of his own hands and in the end realized that these, apart from God, were all meaningless (Ecclesiastes 2:9–11). We don't have to make the same mistakes Solomon made. If we remember that we can't raise our kids apart from God, and we humble ourselves and pray, God will hear our prayers and help us.

> Then the LORD appeared to Solomon in the night and said to him: "I have heard your prayer and have chosen this place for myself as a house of sacrifice. When I shut up the heavens so that there is no rain, or command the locust to devour the land, or send pestilence among my people, if my people who are called by my name humble themselves, and pray and seek my face and turn from their wicked ways, then I will hear from heaven and will forgive their sin and heal their land. Now my eyes will be open and my ears attentive to the prayer that is made in this place." (2 Chronicles 7:12–15)

7. What part of this Scripture passage most encourages you to trust God through prayer? Why?

8. What areas of pride might parents need to repent of?

Relate

I started my parenting journey confident that if I did everything right my kids would turn out fine. I didn't realize it at the time, but God would challenge my self-sufficient attitude with a few trials designed to draw me back into dependence on him. After all, he's the one who supplies our needs and is helping us behind the scenes. Read this account from page 48 in *Parenting First Aid*, and discuss the questions that follow.

> Before conceiving our twins, Lois and I were as prepared for parenting as any couple could be. We both babysat extensively and lived with Christian families. So we sat in the front row, watching others' strengths and weaknesses as parents. I read the most definitive books on parenting available at the time and planned to follow the advice each gave with the military precision I applied to the rest of my life.
>
> As our children grew, life threw us a curveball or two. Potty training humbled me when it didn't work as I had planned. That should have been a sign that I needed God more than the parenting books. But we pressed on, purposing to be good Christian parents and expecting our children to become good Christian kids. We were careful not to expose Emma and Nathan to too much TV or inappropriate programs. They grew up with family worship and (somewhat) daily devotions. We decided to homeschool them so that we could shape their curriculum with a God-centered focus and we enrolled our

twins in our local church homeschool co-op. We sat together as a family in church and looked to help all our kids develop friendships with other children from our church.

Our daughter Emma turned out just like we planned. She wasn't perfect, a bit slow to do work or chores, but she responded well to discipline, and God began to draw her to himself at a young age. She gave her life to Christ in her teen years. She saw how God lifted the weight of sin from the shoulders of others in our church and, in the middle of one night, she went into the bathroom to call out to God. She wouldn't stop until he removed the weight of her sin. God kindly responded with grace, and she left the bathroom a different person. We noticed a difference in her service around the home as she started helping out without being asked. She became a shining star.

Nathan, on the other hand, played the part of a good Christian son on the outside, but inside he was far from God. A sizeable group of his homeschool classmates created an anti-fellowship pact, where they pledged they would never tell on each other, no matter what they did. So, while I slept at night, Nathan was sneaking out of our house to meet up with his other church friends to go drinking in a local park. It wasn't until another family caught one of their kids that we found out that Nathan was involved. I remember crying out to the Lord, pleading my case. "God," I prayed, "I am sleeping at two in the morning! How can I be expected to parent twenty-four hours a day?" We also told our son that he was too young to date, but that didn't stop him. He had a secret girlfriend in his double-life world. To us, she was just a "friend."

Then came the first of several run-ins with the police. I got the call no dad ever wants to receive. "Can you come pick up your son at the station?" He and his girlfriend were taken into custody since they were in a car containing drugs. I felt a wave of relief when I discovered that the police did not charge them, as the drugs belonged to the car's owner. But subsequent run-ins revealed that my son was as involved as any of his other church friends.

"Church kids!" I called out to God, laying out my case for God's unfairness to me. "Lord, we homeschooled them. We did devotions with our kids and family worship. We were careful not to expose them to worldliness, and we limited their friends to other church kids. What more are we supposed to do?"

At that moment God was kind to answer me. I felt a distinct message in the core of my being. The Holy Spirit convicted me of my independence. "I don't want you parenting standing up; I want you parenting kneeling down." The scales fell from my eyes as I realized the pride with which I had parented. That was when Psalm 127:1 gained new meaning: "Unless the LORD builds the house, those who build it labor in vain." I am convinced that God designed my son's trials to humble me. If he had transformed Nathan's life as he had Emma's, I would have become the most self-righteous pastor ever, attributing their success to the work of my hands. God wanted the credit for saving my children; I was looking to keep it for myself.

9. How is the message, "I don't want you parenting standing up; I want you parenting kneeling down," a good lesson for you to learn too?

10. We all know we must trust God for the building of our house, but too often we place our trust in our own parenting wisdom and

work. What part of your parenting wisdom and work are you most tempted to trust instead of God for the success of your children?

Respond

Spend time now in group prayer. Pray for one participant's situation, and for other items springing from this week's study.

Before you leave, plan to take one or more of these *action steps* during the coming week. At the next study session, you'll have a chance to report on how it went.

- List some of the ways God has answered your prayers in the past. How can reviewing this list strengthen your faith for the current challenges you face?

- List your worries on paper in two columns. In the first column, write out the troubles you are experiencing right now. In the second column, write down your worries for tomorrow. Cut the paper in half, tear up the tomorrow side, and toss it in the trash. Then spend time praying for today until God gives you peace that he is with you and will provide.

- One of the best ways to fight worry is to share your fears and concerns with others. Take time to call a friend and confess your unbelief, anxiety, and worry. Ask your friend to join you in prayer and hold you accountable to cast your cares upon the Lord.

- Write out a prayer that asks God for specific help with each of your children. Use it to call out to God with faith that he is able to move on your behalf.

Remember

Memorize Psalm 127:1. "Unless the LORD builds the house, those who build it labor in vain."

A BELIEVING PARENT

Main Idea

A parent's greatest help is trusting in God's Word, the Bible.

To Prepare for Your Study Session

WEEK ONE

Read

Read through chapter 5 of *Parenting First Aid*, which discusses 2 Timothy 1:5 and 3:14–17.

Review

No matter what you are trying to accomplish, it is important to practice the fundamentals. These are the essential, basic skills you must never forget. Even a professional golfer must remember to keep his head down and his eyes on the ball through the swing. The most accomplished of figure skaters can't forget to sharpen her skates before competing. And the most experienced Christian parents need to remember to rely on God's Word to carry them through parenting their kids. If these fundamentals are neglected, the golfer will top the ball, the skater will slip, and the parent will lose faith and become discouraged.

In his short exhortation to Timothy, Paul reminds his seasoned disciple of a few fundamental truths that are applicable to us as parents:

> But as for you, continue in what you have learned and have firmly believed, knowing from whom you learned it and how from childhood you have been acquainted with the sacred writings, which are able to make you wise for salvation through faith in Christ Jesus. All Scripture is breathed out by God and profitable for teaching, for reproof, for correction, and for training in righteousness, that the man of God may be complete, equipped for every good work. (2 Timothy 3:14–17)

Paul reminds Timothy that the Scriptures he learned as a child are breathed out (authored) by God and are therefore powerful to save the lost and give us the wisdom we need to live day to day. Paul knew that these fundamental truths are easy to forget. So when we as parents experience a trial with our son or daughter, we need to be sure never to forget God's powerful Word lest we become discouraged and slip into worry, fear, unbelief, and anger. For the one who has studied the Bible, the Holy Spirit is able to use what we've learned or memorized to encourage us in times of trial.

Reflect

Answer these questions as you read through chapter 5 in *Parenting First Aid*, or when you finish. Write your answers down so you can discuss them later, if you want, when you meet with your group.

1. What part of Paul's encouragement to Timothy do you most need to hear as a parent?

2. How can Paul's testimony build our faith for what God can do in the lives of even our most rebellious children?

3. In what situations are you prone to forget the importance of the gospel fundamentals, like sharing the good news of Jesus with your children and praying that God would use his words to transform their lives?

4. When you feel like you are not good at sharing the gospel, what might you do to remember and trust that the gospel works by God's power, not your presentation?

WEEK TWO

Read

In *Parenting First Aid*, read through chapter 6, which contains encouragements from Lamentations 3:16–17.

Review

Every morning, God pours out fresh mercies upon our new day. But to walk in those mercies, we must keep our focus on God. That is why we should start our day lifting our gaze upon God, his character, and his promises. The writer of Lamentations encourages Israel to remember God's mercies despite one of their most horrific trials, the fall of Jerusalem.

Rather than look first to our trials and hardships only to be freshly discouraged, let's look to God. God is able to save. God is able to restore. God is able to transform. Through life's most difficult trials we must always remember God is able, God is able. God gives us mercy for each day, one day at a time. Fresh mercies flood our soul when we realize that every day is a fresh opportunity to hope in God. When God refreshes us through his Word and sustains us by his grace, we have hope for another day. Hope for tomorrow helps us respond to our children in love today, and that is often the way God reaches them.

Reflect

Answer these questions as you read through chapter 6 of *Parenting First Aid*. You'll be able to share some of your responses, if you want, when your study session meets.

5. How does knowing that the familiar phrase, "God's mercies are new every morning," was spoken in the midst of great tragedy give it greater meaning for your trials?

6. A lament is an honest prayer to God about the difficulties we face. How can you draw comfort from knowing God welcomes prayers of lament?

7. If you were going to write your own lament, what season of life or time of trial would you write it about?

Study Session

Begin this session by reviewing the action steps from the end of the last study. Which steps did you take? What did you learn, or how were you encouraged?

Now go through the reflection questions for this study that you answered during the past few weeks. Pick some of them to discuss, or let participants share the answers that were most meaningful to them. Then continue with the rest of this study.

Refuel

Matthew tells us that after the Last Supper, before leaving for the Mount of Olives, Jesus and the disciples sang a hymn (Matthew 26:30). Custom would suggest they sang through the Hallel (Psalms

113 through 118), which was traditionally sung throughout the Pass-over meal.

As you read through the opening verses of Psalm 116, imagine Jesus singing these words to his Father just before the crucifixion. With the full knowledge of the suffering to come, Jesus declared his love for the Lord and repeated the psalmist's plea for mercy. Only no mercy would come for Jesus. God the Father would turn his face away from his Son so that he would never turn his face away from us. Jesus's rejection made the way for our salvation and help in all of life, including our parenting. God denied him mercy in order to pour out his mercy on us and our children. So meditate on these words with fresh faith that God will hear your prayers and answer you.

> I love the LORD, because he has heard
> my voice and my pleas for mercy.
> Because he inclined his ear to me,
> therefore I will call on him as long as I live.
> The snares of death encompassed me;
> the pangs of Sheol laid hold on me;
> I suffered distress and anguish.
> Then I called on the name of the LORD:
> "O LORD, I pray, deliver my soul!" (Psalm 116:1–4)

8. How does knowing that Jesus likely sang these words to his Father give them meaning for your parenting today?

9. What part of these verses most encourages your soul to wait upon God's mercy? Explain why.

Relate

I first began pastoring Maria and Gabe after his cancer diagnosis. Gabe and Maria were faithful parents with an evangelistic ministry to children. Gabe worked hard up north in his cleaning business most of the year and then spent the winter with his family in Florida ministering to children. So when I learned of their son Destin's rebellion and watched him spiral out of control, I was confused. *God, what are you doing?* I wondered. We prayed, but things got worse. Still, Maria never wavered, and it was her trust in the Scriptures she read and memorized and his fresh mercies every morning that held her steady through it all. Read her story, from page 73 of *Parenting First Aid*, below.

> That winter marked the beginning of Maria's years of lament. Destin's rebellion grew steadily, much as cancer took hold of his father. Gabe fought his cancer valiantly while he did his best to speak Scripture and warnings to his son, but Gabe didn't win either war. He died less than a year later, in early September, leaving Maria alone to parent their three children. Destin loved his father, and after Gabe died, Destin was devastated. He went wild, drowning himself in alcohol and further drug use.
>
> In the years that followed, Destin barely graduated high school, then experimented with harder drugs and became hopelessly addicted to heroin. He traveled from rehab to jail to halfway houses to the street and back to jail. Maria lost

count of the times Destin went to rehab. Each time he hit bottom, she shared the same message, "I would tell him that God is doing this, he wants your heart. He is not going to let you go. He wants to save you." Destin flatly rejected her counsel saying, "I don't want that, Mom."

"At the end of the day when I laid my head on the pillow," Maria remembers, "I was scared and anxious and really had to calm myself down to even be able to sleep. I slept with my wallet, phone, and car keys under my pillow so Destin couldn't take them. I would pray and cry out to God for help." She always remembered the Scripture that God's mercies were new every morning. She said, "I felt fresh and thought there was hope. God would get me through the night, give me peace to be able to sleep, and I would just wake up with hope. Though at times I also had fear, I knew that God was going to get us through."

It wasn't until eight years later, with Destin in prison facing serious jail time, that he finally gave his life to Christ. With a video hearing coming up, Destin was afraid. His counselor said he'd had too many chances, wasted too many rehabs, and needed to stay in prison. After a phone call from his mom, Destin got down on his knees in his cell and called out to Christ to save him. He prayed along with his mom for mercy. The next day, rather than sentence him to prison, the judge miraculously extended mercy to Destin and allowed him to attend a seven-month program with Teen Challenge. At that moment, Destin knew that God was helping him, but days after the program ended seven months later, he continued his struggle with drugs. While God had turned Destin's heart, the addiction yet enslaved him. It would be another three years before Destin's battle with drugs finally came to an end.

Through those long years, Maria never lost hope for her son and never lost sight of the fact that the Lord is good to those who wait for him. His mercies were poured fresh out on Maria each morning. She was convinced that the salvation of the Lord would come. She wrote Destin while he spent time in prison, recovery, and shelters. Here is a sample of the many letters and emails she wrote.

Destin,

"A righteous man who walks in his integrity.
How blessed are his sons after him." Proverbs 20:7

I think of Dad when I read these verses and what a man of integrity he was. Then, I remember how God has spared you from many dangers and destruction. You are blessed, and God has protected you and guarded your life! I can only believe that he has a call on your life and that he is using this time to strengthen your faith. He is going to make a mighty warrior of God from your broken life, just like he did for your dad. Dad's strength came from his utter trust in God. Jesus set him free from his lifestyle of destruction, and he will do the same for you.

When we talked on the phone last night, and you told me about the panic attack, I thought of 1 Peter 5:6–7: "Humble yourselves under God's mighty hand, that he might lift you up in due time. *Cast all your anxiety on him, for he cares for you*" and how God's Word is powerful. (Well, I admit, that's not the first thing I thought—at first, I panicked, too! ☺) When Dad was sick and dying, we meditated on verses to keep our minds strong through the trial. I believe that is what God is calling you to do. Meditate on the Word of God and anxious thoughts will have to leave. I also get barraged with anxiety and God's Word is a comfort.

My prayer for you:
Thank you that you are breaking Destin's will and conforming it to yours. I pray that you would help him yield to this painful process. I pray that it

would yield much lasting fruit, in his life and in the lives of others around him. I pray that you would use him to be a light to the poor and the addict and that he would be a testimony of your mercy and grace. Pour out your Spirit upon him and give him power to endure. Cause much growth in him as he reads your words and meditates on you. I pray for complete deliverance of drugs, alcohol, gambling, nicotine, lust, and all manner of evil and that he would be a man of God with a heart after you. Bring healing to his body and soul. Comfort him, hold him and keep him by your sustaining grace. Help him to see the bright future you have for him—a godly wife, a family and spiritual leadership. We look forward to all you will do in this young man's life. In the precious name of Jesus, AMEN!

I love you, Destin Mark!
Mom

10. What part of Maria's struggle with Destin most affects you, and why?

11. How can reading about Maria's faith for Destin encourage you as you walk through your trials?

Respond

Spend time now in group prayer. Pray for one participant's situation, and for other items springing from this week's study.

Before you leave, plan to take one or more of these *action steps* during the coming week. At the next study session, you'll have a chance to report on how it went.

- Read Lamentations 3:25–26 and allow it to bolster your faith as you wait for God's salvation for your children or his help in their trials.
- Take time to pray through one of the psalms of lament (Psalms 42, 57, 77, 86, and 89) that speak of God's mercy, faithfulness, and steadfast love. Ask God to meet you through the words you pray.
- Write your own prayer of lament to the Lord, and trust God to hear you as you use it to call out to him for deliverance.

Remember

Memorize Lamentations 3:22–23. "The steadfast love of the Lord never ceases; his mercies never come to an end; they are new every morning; great is your faithfulness."

A PRAYING PARENT

Main Idea

Prayer is our doorway to peace in the midst of our trials.

To Prepare for Your Study Session

WEEK ONE

Read

Reflect on Philippians 4:4–13 by reading chapter 7 of *Parenting First Aid* during your first week.

Review

Have you ever wondered if God hears your prayers for your children? Well, Scripture answers that question. Peter tells us that God's ears are open to our prayers (1 Peter 3:12), and John said, "We know that he hears us" (1 John 5:15). One of the most amazing gifts God has given us as parents is the promise that he hears our prayers. He actually encourages us to come to him with our anxious thoughts and worries, and he will give us peace. Imagine, the God who spoke the universe into existence with a few words invites us to lift up our troubles in prayer to him!

Add to that invitation the certain fact that God is good and cannot lie, and you realize how valuable Philippians 4:7 is when it says, "Do not be anxious about anything, but in everything by prayer and supplication with thanksgiving let your requests be made known to God. And the peace of God, which surpasses all understanding, will guard your hearts and your mind in Christ Jesus" (Philippians 4:6–7). Here is God's promise: Lift up your prayer to me and I will replace your anxiety with peace.

So why do we struggle? Perhaps it's because we don't just want God's peace, we want our parenting trials to dissolve and disappear. But God doesn't promise to take all our trials away. He promises to work our trials for our good and to guard our hearts and minds while he uses those trials to make us more like Christ.

Reflect

After you read through chapter 7 in *Parenting First Aid*, or as you go, answer the questions below. You'll have an opportunity to discuss them when you meet with your group.

1. Read through the list of Paul's sufferings in 2 Corinthians 11:25–28. How does knowing what Paul went through make his call to cast your anxieties on God (Philippians 4:6–7) more compelling?

2. Consider the common parenting concerns listed below. Which of them do you need to mention to God more often, and why?

   • Anxiety over your child's health or safety
   • Anxiety over your child's behavior
   • Anxiety over your child's performance

- Anxiety over your child's spiritual life
- Anxiety over your own abilities as a parent
- Your tendency to try to control your child
- Your tendency to get angry with your child
- Your habit of withdrawing from your child or avoiding some parental duties
- Your over-concern with how others might judge your parenting
- Parenting tension between you and your spouse or another family member
- Other: _____

3. Of the verses from Philippians listed in day two's devotion on page 81 (Philippians 1:6; 1:19; 2:12–13; 3:8, 13–14; 3:20–4:1), which encourages you most? Why?

4. How often do you tell your anxieties to someone else? Whom might you ask to pray with you and for you?

WEEK TWO

Read

Read the devotions in chapter 8 of *Parenting First Aid*, which build on Isaiah 1:1–20.

Review

You won't find a ton of stories of successful, trial-free parenting in the Scriptures. Right from Genesis and the fall we see how sin ruins God's good plan: Cain murders his brother Abel and soon the generations which come after them rebel against God. Is it any wonder we experience the same challenges in raising our children? The gospel is our only source of hope for the transformation of our children.

This is especially evident in Isaiah 1, where we learn that God himself dealt with rebellious children. We know God is a perfectly faithful parent, and so we learn that perfect parenting doesn't ensure that our sinful children will obey. It is only through God's gospel plan that God's children are redeemed and their sinful hearts washed clean. So why are we so surprised when our children go astray? Part of the challenge is that people broadcast their parenting successes but hide their challenges. This gives the impression that most parents have it together and don't experience trials and challenges. It is into this that God opens up to us his own heart as he parented sinful Israel.

Reflect

As you read through chapter 8 of *Parenting First Aid*, answer the questions below. If you want, you'll be able to share some of your responses when your study session meets.

5. How are the sins of Israel described in Isaiah 1 similar to your struggles and those of your children?

6. God related to Israel with grace and kindness. How can his mercy encourage you when it comes to how you approach your children? Give an example.

7. Think of a time when you became weary in parenting. How can knowing that God described himself as a weary parent (Isaiah 1:14) comfort and help you through a difficult parenting season?

8. Think of at least two reasons why it's important that a struggling parent know the truth expressed in Isaiah 1:18. How does that verse foretell the gospel announced in 1 John 1:5–9?

Study Session

Begin this session by reviewing the action steps from the end of the last study. Did you read the psalms of lament, or write your own lament? What did you learn, or how were you encouraged?

Now go through the reflection questions for this study that you answered during the past few weeks. Pick some of them to discuss, or let participants share the answers that were most meaningful to them. Then continue with the rest of this study.

Refuel

Jeremiah 29:11–14 is often taken out of context as a blanket promise that God will deliver us out of every trial instantly. But that is not the message of the text. Jeremiah speaks this prophecy just after he drops the difficult news that Israel will remain in captivity in Babylon for seventy years (see verse 10). Hananiah had just prophesied that the Lord would deliver Israel in two years (Jeremiah 28:3–4)

God sends Jeremiah to tell the people Hananiah's prophecy is a lie (Jeremiah 28:15). It is in this context that Jeremiah delivers the hope-filled words we read. The hope of Jeremiah 29:11–14 is not that all our troubles will quickly vanish, but rather that God will walk with us through our trial and will in his perfect time bring it to an end. So meditate on this verse and know that your trial will only last as long as God allows, and that while you are in it you can cry out to God and find him, and he will comfort you.

> "For I know the plans I have for you, declares the LORD, plans for welfare and not for evil, to give you a future and a hope. Then you will call upon me and come and pray to me, and I will hear you. You will seek me and find me, when you seek me with all your heart. I will be found by you, declares the LORD, and I will restore your fortunes and gather you from all the nations and all the places where I have driven you, declares the LORD, and I will bring you back to the place from which I sent you into exile." (Jeremiah 29:11–14)

9. Consider the fact that God's promise is not to end your troubles immediately but to use them for your good and be with you through them. How might this change what you pray for your children, and for your parenting?

10. What is God's chief goal for his people in the Jeremiah passage, and what might your parenting look like if it is your goal for your children as well?

Relate

I had the privilege of witnessing a Billy Graham crusade and watching the people stream out of their seats in response to the gospel. Billy Graham lived his whole life in service to God and finished well in the end. That is something so seldom done, even among godly men. If there ever were a parent that you might think could raise a godly son, it's Billy Graham, but even the twentieth century's most beloved evangelist couldn't make his son, William Franklin Graham III, a Christian. Read Franklin's story, which comes from page 97 in *Parenting First Aid*.

Franklin (that's what his parents decided to call him to distinguish him from his father) was all boy. He grew up a thrillseeker who loved anything fast, from cars to motorcycles. He describes himself as a rebel in search of a cause. Though he "made a decision for Christ" at age eight,[1] he didn't experience genuine conversion until his early twenties.

As you would expect, Franklin was surrounded by the same love for Christ in private that Billy Graham preached in the pulpit. His father was a man of integrity and he saw it firsthand. Franklin describes his upbringing: "My parents never crammed religion down my throat. They did try to instill in all of us kids the importance of a personal relationship with God. Every evening our family had devotions before we went to bed. Mama or Daddy would read a short passage from the

---

1   Franklin Graham, *Rebel with a Cause* (Nashville: Thomas Nelson, 1995), 122.

Bible, and then we would each say a sentence prayer. In the morning, after breakfast, Mama or Daddy would lead us in prayer before we left the house for school. It didn't matter who was in the house at the time—our housekeeper, caretaker or guests—it was something everyone did in our home. I can't remember a day when this didn't happen."[2]

Though his father was gone for months at a time, he gave himself to caring for his son when he returned from long crusades. Franklin's mind is full of fond memories of hiking, camping, and going on special trips with his father—even traveling with his dad to meet the President of the United States. Franklin understood the importance of his father's work and never doubted the sincerity of his faith. While his dad traveled, God was kind enough to provide strong Christian role models for Franklin, and he was surrounded by examples of the transformative power of the gospel. Christianity wasn't phony to him; he just decided he wouldn't play by the rules and would live life his way, as a rebel.

He started smoking in grade school and continually lied about it to his parents. He drank, dated unbelievers, drove without a license, evaded the police on a high-speed chase, stayed out as late as he wanted to while listening to rock-and-roll music. Franklin drank beer, got into fights at school, didn't take his studies seriously, barely graduated high school, and was expelled from college. He lived to torment his sisters, his parents, and his teachers and wouldn't let anyone tell him what to do.

He describes his years in boarding school. "I took pride in my individuality and tried to see how far I could stretch rules before getting reprimanded. Many of these infractions were minor, but everything added to my rebellion. Instead of getting my esteem from achieving within the system, I got my thrills and identity from challenging the system. I was following the classic pattern of every rebel."[3]

---

2   Ibid., 7–8.
3   Ibid., 41.

In spite of Franklin's poor behavior, his mother and father always reached out in love. Their demonstration of God's love often surprised him. His confrontations with his parents never resulted in them becoming bitter. In fact, Franklin thought his parents were cool and described them tenderly: "My parents made it clear what they would accept or reject in my values and behavior. But on the other hand, they never squashed my individuality or demeaned me as a person. They knew much more clearly than I did the pressures I faced being a 'preacher's kid' as well as the oldest son of a 'Christian Legend.' I'm sure God gave them wisdom to know that if they pushed me too hard to conform, I might take off running and never come back—not just away from them, but perhaps from God too."[4]

By the time Franklin was twenty, he smoked heavily and drank often. But his sinful life was leaving him empty and unsatisfied. He felt miserable because he knew his life wasn't right with God. He witnessed God answering prayers anytime he involved himself in any part of the ministry that was his father's life.

On his twenty-second birthday, Billy took a walk with his son and gave him a personal evangelistic appeal. God used the same appeal that drove thousands to their knees in football stadiums, now laser-focused on one boy's heart. "Franklin," his father said, "your mother and I sense there's a struggle going on in your life. You're going to have to make a choice either to accept Christ or reject him. You can't continue to play the middle ground. Either you're going to choose to follow and obey him or reject him.

"I want you to know we're proud of you, Franklin. We love you no matter what you do in life and no matter where you go. The door of our home is always open, and you're always welcome. But you're going to have to make a choice."[5]

---

4   Ibid., 53.
5   Ibid., 119–20.

After being confronted by a friend a few days later and with his father's words still haunting him, Franklin got down on his knees and surrendered his life to Jesus. Franklin describes that moment. "I put my cigarette out and got down on my knees beside my bed. I'm not sure what I prayed, but I know that I poured my heart out to God and confessed my sin. I told him I was sorry and that if he would take the pieces of my life and somehow put them back together, I was his. I wanted to live my life for him from that day forward. I asked him to forgive me and cleanse me and I invited him by faith to come into my life. My years of running and rebellion had ended. I got off my knees and went to bed. It was finished. The rebel had found the cause."[6]

There is no doubt that God used the Graham family's daily devotions, the godly example of his parents, the testimony of answered prayer, and the witness of the solid Christian men who befriended him in the years when his father was away. But none of those good things could save Franklin in and of themselves. Those spiritual influences didn't stop Franklin from smoking, drinking, lying, or doing whatever he wanted. But his parents were not trusting in themselves or these good works to save their son. They were trusting in God and had faith to believe God would apprehend their son. That was evidenced by the countless prayers they offered on his behalf. "Franklin didn't have a chance," they wrote in the afterword of his biography. "He had been given to God before his birth, and God has kept his hand on him without letting up all these years."[7]

11. How does knowing that even Billy Graham had challenges in parenting encourage or discourage you?

---

6   Ibid., 123.
7   Ibid., 314.

12. What can we do when we face parenting trials like Billy and Ruth did?

Respond

Spend time now in group prayer. Pray for one participant's situation, and for other items springing from this week's study.

Before you leave, plan to take one or both of these *action steps* during the coming week. At the next study session, you'll have a chance to report on how it went.

- How well are you handling the anxieties that stem from your parenting trials? When in the next day could you set aside time to cry out to God and cast your anxieties on him? Add it to your schedule and follow through.
- Too often our children hear more about what they need to do to change than they do about the promise that God can change them. When could you share the grace and mercy represented by Isaiah 1:18 with your son or daughter?

Remember

Memorize Isaiah 1:18. "Come now, let us reason together, says the LORD: though your sins are like scarlet, they shall be as white as snow; though they are red like crimson, they shall become like wool."

DISCUSSION 5

A PATIENT PARENT

Main idea

In the midst of our parenting trials, it is important to remember that saving our children is God's job.

To Prepare for Your Study Session

WEEK ONE

Read

During your first week of preparing for your study session, work through chapter 9 of *Parenting First Aid*. The chapter discusses 1 Corinthians 3:6–7, Luke 1:8–17, and Hebrews 8:8–12.

Review

Our job as parents is one of seed planting and watering. We plant the seed of the gospel by sharing the gospel story with our children and demonstrating what a life lived for Christ looks like. We water the seed of the gospel through our prayers for our children and our love toward them. But after that, we must wait, like patient farmers do every planting season, for God to cause the seed we planted to grow. Sprouting that gospel seed is above our pay grade.

When our children are young we rely on discipline to change their behavior, but as our kids grow we soon discover that only God changes their hearts. He is the one who promised to take their rebellious hearts of stone away and give them hearts of flesh that grow in obedience to him. God is the one who writes his law upon our kids' hearts and restores them in relationship, first to himself and then to us.

Reflect

Answer these questions as you read through chapter 9, or once you finish. Write out your answers and be ready to refer to them when your study session meets.

1. What is your role in the conversion of your children? What is God's role? What tends to happen in your life when you fail to keep those roles straight? Explain.

   • I feel condemnation if my children rebel.
   • I get controlling or overbearing toward my children.
   • Telling the gospel to my children becomes a moment of anxiety rather than a message of joy.
   • I neglect to pray.
   • Other (explain)

2. How does the twin hope from Luke 1:17, that God will turn your children's hearts to you and your heart to them, encourage you? What changes do you long to see God work?

3. How can Hebrews 8:8–12, which says God puts his law on his people's minds and hearts, encourage you when your kids struggle? Give a specific example if you can.

WEEK TWO

Read

Study Romans 8:26–39 by reading chapter 10 in *Parenting First Aid*.

Review

Paul teaches us in Romans 8 that God is never off the job and is always in control. Not only that, the Spirit is at work interceding for you (v. 26) and so is Jesus (v. 34)! Do you ever wonder if your prayers are too weak to arouse the mighty hand of God? Should doubt creep in, remember that the Spirit and the Son are interceding for you so that all things work together for your good. Always! Events may not unfold in keeping with your desired timeline, but you must fight to believe they will work out for your good in God's timing.

Reflect

Write down your answers to these questions that go with chapter 10 in *Parenting First Aid*. You'll be discussing some of them when your study session meets.

4. Where do you need faith to believe that God can work all things together for your family's good? Make a list of those areas and then pray through the list, asking God to work these things together for your family's good and to give you faith to believe that he can.

5. Why does Paul use the gospel (God giving his Son to die for us) as the logical reason to prove that God the Father will graciously give us all things? How might you use the same reasoning to help you trust God?

6. How can remembering that Jesus was tempted like you build your confidence that he is sympathetic to your challenges?

7. Are there areas of your life, or parenting failures, that you've been convinced separate you from the love of God? Any that suggest that you don't qualify for his promises? If so, confess your unbelief as sin and make a fresh commitment to believe the truths in Romans 8.

Study Session

Begin this session by reviewing the action steps from the end of the last study. Did you set aside time with God or share Isaiah 1:18 with your kids? What did you learn, or how were you encouraged?

Now go through the reflection questions for this study that you answered during the past few weeks. Pick some of them to discuss, or let each participant share the answers that were most meaningful to them. Then continue with the rest of this study.

Refuel

Paul's teaching on taking up the armor of God (Ephesians 6:10–20) has encouraged Christians through the centuries like few other passages. When life's challenges confront us, we can feel helpless. It is so kind of God to give us something we can do while we wait for him to move. We take up the shield of faith, which is our belief and trust that God is able to work on our behalf, and we engage in prayer, knowing that God hears us.

So when we are weary from the battle, we can find fresh faith in Paul's exhortation. We wrestle with spiritual forces warring against us (v. 12), but the flaming darts of the enemy will not penetrate our shield of faith and God's Word will strengthen us until our prayers are answered.

In all circumstances take up the shield of faith, with which you can extinguish all the flaming darts of the evil one; and take the helmet of salvation, and the sword of the Spirit, which is the word of God, praying at all times in the Spirit, with all prayer and supplication. To that end, keep alert with all perseverance, making supplication for all the saints. (Ephesians 6:16–18)

8. Which pieces of "armor" seem especially necessary for you as a parent, and why?

9. What are the accusations and lies the enemy uses (the flaming darts) to discourage you? What can you do to neutralize them?

Relate

I can remember Destin's longstanding struggles over the years. Whenever I'd look at my appointment calendar and see his mother Maria's name listed, I would wrestle with God over what I should tell her. *Keep keeping the faith, and trust God* sounded insufficient to me. My own faith grew tired and yet, again and again, I would encourage Maria with the truth that God has the power to save and deliver her son and will work all his trials out for good—even a gunshot to the back. And that is exactly what God did. Read the story below, which comes from page 109 in *Parenting First Aid*.

> A few months after starting Teen Challenge rehab, Destin's life seemed to turn a corner. He, along with ten other men, were getting saturated with good biblical teaching and worship six hours a day, and it was paying off. This focus on God, away from the temptations of the drug scene, worked wonders for him. I met with Destin's mother, Maria, during that time and I remember her saying that she finally had her son back.
>
> While Destin truly believed that Jesus was real and God forgave his sins, he wasn't strong enough to resist the temptations that assaulted him back in the real world. Once out of Teen Challenge, he found it difficult to believe that he could find his joy and satisfaction in living for Jesus alone. Recalling those days, he said, "When I got out of Teen Challenge, I began gambling on sports and playing poker, and that took away my desire for the Word of God. It was only a couple of months before I was back on heroin, and it got way worse than before. Because I had tasted Jesus and knew he was real, the shame was much greater. More drugs were needed to take away the feelings of guilt and shame. It was a horrible existence, to know God and continue in sin."
>
> The resulting chaos brought Maria back into my pastoral office. After multiple rehabs, a prison conversion, and the better part of a year in the mountains of Pennsylvania for Destin, there were no easy answers. Maria had exhausted every earthly avenue available to help her son. But God wasn't ready to give up on Destin. He planned to use the very drug underworld that enslaved Destin to free him from his slavery. Destin recounts the story:
>
> > I grew up hearing the gospel of Jesus every day of my life, memorizing Bible verses, homeschooling, going

to church, acting in church plays, and spending time with my family. That was my life. When I turned twelve, my desires changed. I wanted friends, wanted to be liked, and wanted to feel good. Although I was still around church and heard about Jesus all the time, I didn't care about him. I thought that joy was found outside of Jesus and that I was tricked into believing in Jesus so that I wouldn't be a bad kid.

Soon, I found friends that partied. Within days, I was completely enslaved to feeling good and forgetting about my problems. My journey of bondage and slavery began. As the years went by, the drugs got harder, the consequences were steeper, and the pleasure was diminishing to nothing. At nineteen years old, I was completely dependent on heroin and could not stop. Ephesians 2 talks about us being dead in sin, following the course of this world, following Satan, and carrying out the desires of the body and the mind. That was my life: I do what I want when I want, and I don't care what the result is. Jesus said, "Everyone who commits sin is a slave to sin." I was a dead slave.

In July 2014, as a last-ditch effort to get clean after I failed to stay off of drugs following a seven-month Teen Challenge program, I moved to Allentown to try to "start over." I found drugs within a couple of days. A week later, I was going to meet my drug dealer, and he pulled out a .38 handgun, pointed it at my face, and said, "Don't run." The physical craving for heroin combined with the hopelessness in my soul compelled me to try to get away. He fired one shot at me point blank, and it hit me in the spine. There I was, on my back looking at the sky, bleeding to death in a dark back alley. I remember thinking, *I'm about to go meet my Creator, and I don't know what I'm going to say.* Instinctively, I started to scream the name of Jesus. The bullet went through my lung and stomach so I couldn't breathe, but I just kept gasping, "JESUS, SAVE ME!!!" Within seconds I heard sirens, and the EMTs scooped me off the ground into an ambulance. Then it just went black.

Jesus heard my cry, and he saved me. I lived out the plea of Psalm 116:

> I love the LORD, because he has heard
>   my voice and my pleas for mercy.
> Because he inclined his ear to me,
>   therefore I will call on him as long as I live.
> The snares of death encompassed me;
>   the pangs of Sheol laid hold on me;
> I suffered distress and anguish.
>   Then I called on the name of the LORD:
>   "O LORD, I pray, deliver my soul!"
> Gracious is the LORD, and righteous;
>   our God is merciful.
> The LORD preserves the simple;
>   when I was brought low, he saved me.
> Return, O my soul, to your rest;
>   for the LORD has dealt bountifully with you.
> For you have delivered my soul from death,
>   my eyes from tears,
>   my feet from stumbling;
> I will walk before the LORD
>   in the land of the living. (Psalm 116:1–9)

When I awoke, I was completely overcome with the love of God. Why would he do this for someone like me, who just kept running from him? It became real that God loved me, and it was not based on my performance, it was in spite of it. My faith was quickly put into action as I told the nurses to take me off the painkillers. I wanted to be free.

In the days and weeks spent recovering on his mother's couch, Destin read the Bible all day long. He memorized the book of James and several psalms. That study completely changed his perspective. God set Destin free from his slavery to chemicals by opening his eyes to glimpse of the deep, deep love of Jesus.

Destin concludes, "Life in Christ is more rewarding and fulfilling than I could have ever imagined, and as I continue to get to know my heavenly Father more day by day, the joy just keeps increasing. God has saved and transformed me, the chief of sinners, and he has the power to rescue and save ANYONE! There is no one on this planet that is too far gone for God to save through the cross of Jesus Christ. Everyone who calls on the name of the Lord will be saved. When you cry to Jesus, he WILL hear you and answer your cry for help!"

No parent would ever write a script for their child's life that included getting shot as the means to deliver them from drugs. Yet when Maria watches Destin share God's Word with others struggling as he once did, she wouldn't turn back the clock to avoid the shooting. She can see how God used those dark moments to transform her son's life. God alone is the one who knows how to weave a person's story into the fabric of his purpose and kingdom. That is why turning the hearts of our children is God's job.

10. Maria endured ten long years before her son Destin finally broke his addiction to drugs. How can her story of perseverance and the stories of other parents like her spur us on to believe God for our children?

11. How has God used your trials to grow your perseverance and faith?

Respond

Spend time in group prayer. Pray for one participant's situation, and for other items springing from this week's study.

Before you leave, plan to take one or more of these *action steps* during the coming week. At the next study session, you'll have a chance to report on how it went.

- Look up the following verses to help you articulate the gospel message:

  John 3:16
  Romans 10:9–13
  1 Corinthians 15:3–4
  1 Peter 3:18
  Titus 3:3–7

  If you memorize these verses, you will always be equipped to share the gospel with your children. You will never need to say, "I don't know what to say."

- Are there any situations where you are not sure how or what to pray? List them and ask the Spirit to hear the groaning of your heart and intercede for you.

- What would it look like for you to approach God's throne with confidence? Act on your answer and make your requests known to God.
- Read Romans 8:26–39 out loud as a prayer to God, lifting your eyes to heaven. Pray these words with the confidence that they are the inerrant Word of God. Then add your prayer for your family and the challenges you face, doing so with the confidence that comes from believing the Scriptures we've studied.

Remember

Memorize Romans 8:28. "And we know that for those who love God all things work together for good, for those who are called according to his purpose."

DISCUSSION 6

A DEPENDENT PARENT

Main Idea

God our Shepherd has not abandoned us in our trials.

To Prepare for Your Study Session

WEEK ONE

Read

Read chapter 11 in *Parenting First Aid* during your first week. The key Bible texts are Isaiah 41:8–13, John 14:18–23, and Revelation 20:1–4.

Review

There is one fiery dart the enemy shoots at us that is worse than all others: he claims *God has abandoned you.* In the midst of difficult parenting trials, we can be more easily tempted to think that God has abandoned us. We can feel all alone when our prayers seem unanswered and our trials continue unabated.

But God never leaves or forsakes us. He is always with us. And when we are walking through fiery trials that seem to resist all remedy, it is critical that we rehearse the Scriptures that tell us God is with us. Christians should not find their strength in improving circumstances;

we must locate our faith in the God who controls our circumstances. That way, when circumstances improve we praise God, but we can also praise him when they continue, for he is always with us and he is able to help us.

Reflect

Answer these questions as you read through chapter 11, or once you finish. Write out your answers and be ready to refer to them when your study session meets.

1. Imagine that Isaiah is prophesying to you directly through Isaiah 41:8–13. Where could you use strength and help? Offer these areas in prayer to God, appealing to the promises in Isaiah's prophecy.

2. It can be difficult to believe that God is with us when we go through trials. Which of the following statements describes why you sometimes don't believe God is with you? Explain.

   - It feels like life should get better if God is with me. When it doesn't, I wonder where he is.
   - I can't accept that it's normal for God to use troubles for my good, to grow my faith.
   - I can't accept that God might put my children through trials for their good. I want their lives to be trouble-free.
   - It's hard to believe when I can't see God or understand his reasons.
   - It's easier for me to believe in things I can see and do for myself, like _____.
   - I believe God is able, but I'm not sure he wants to do good for me because _____.

- I feel God won't be with me unless I first _____.
- Other (explain)

3. How does the closeness Moses felt with God, or the glory of the Spirit filling the temple, help you to appreciate the amazing gift we have in the presence of the Holy Spirit in the life of every believer?

4. How has God used trials to help you see that the promises of this earthly life are empty?

WEEK TWO

Read

Read chapter 12 in *Parenting First Aid* during your second week. The key Bible texts are Matthew 18:10–14 and Luke 15:3–7, 11–32.

Review

As our children grow, we need to trust God to watch over them and keep them safe. Years ago, kids would leave their homes during the school year and walk to the bus stop where they would wait with the other neighborhood kids to catch the bus. Today, many parents drive their children to the bus stop and wait with them in the car for the bus to arrive. People say times have changed and it is not safe to leave your kids on their own. Driving our kids to the bus stop provides a sense of security that we lose when they get older and start making decisions on their own. Teens stay out late and begin to make independent choices. Not all of them are wise. It is easy to worry when they make foolish choices and wander from the faith. But we can draw strength from remembering that God is a shepherd who goes after the lost sheep. It's not up to us and we can't drive them everywhere to keep them safe. Jesus taught us that he is the Good Shepherd who goes after the lost. He is the Sovereign God who can bring them home when they stray.

Reflect

Answer the questions below as you read through chapter 12 or once you finish. You'll have a chance to share some answers when your study session meets.

5. How should knowing that God will not let a single one of his children perish and that he can reach your child encourage your faith for your wayward children?

6. How should the parable about the shepherd going after the lost
   sheep encourage you when you doubt God's ability or willingness
   to save your children?

7. How are you encouraged by the parable of the prodigal son? In
   what ways are you challenged to be more like the father in the
   parable?

Study Session

Begin this session by reviewing the action steps from the end of the
last study. Which steps did you take? What did you learn, or how were
you encouraged?

Now go through the reflection questions for this study that you
answered during the past few weeks. Pick some of them to discuss, or
let each participant share the answers that were most meaningful to
them. Then continue with the rest of this study.

Refuel

When the disciples asked Jesus to teach them to pray (Luke 11:1),
he gave them the Lord's Prayer. Matthew's account of that moment

includes a very interesting instruction. Jesus taught that we don't have to "heap up empty phrases" (Matthew 6:7). In other words, God is not in heaven holding us hostage to a word count or time quota of prayer before he hears us. The prayer *Jesus, help me!* is not overlooked by God because it is short.

Do you ever feel that you have not prayed enough? If so, then take comfort with the way Jesus taught his disciples to pray. We are not to put our faith in our prayer—how long or how eloquently we pray; we are to put our faith in the God to whom we pray. As for eloquence, we are allowed to simply copy the very same words Jesus instructed us to pray:

> And when you pray, do not heap up empty phrases as the Gentiles do, for they think that they will be heard for their many words. Do not be like them, for your Father knows what you need before you ask him. Pray then like this:
>
> "Our Father in heaven,
> hallowed be your name.
> Your kingdom come,
> your will be done,
>   on earth as it is in heaven.
> Give us this day our daily bread,
> and forgive us our debts,
>   as we also have forgiven our debtors.
> And lead us not into temptation,
>   but deliver us from evil." (Matthew 6:7–13)

8. Why do you sometimes feel your prayers are inadequate?

9. How can you personalize the Lord's Prayer to fit some common parenting situations? Think of a few and try it.

Relate

Christopher was only a toddler when I started attending our church. His parents were foundational members, a part of the church-planting team that began with a dozen others. I watched him grow up and, after God called me into ministry, I became his children's pastor, then youth pastor, and officiated his wedding. Walking him and his wife through the trial of losing a baby was one of the saddest events of my life. And yet, seeing God's shepherding hand love them through their darkest night demonstrated God's love and care in a way I will never forget. Read their story (from page 134 in *Parenting First Aid*) together, and answer the questions.

> Christopher and Nancy knew something was seriously wrong when their ultrasound technician quietly left the room to get the doctor. A moment later, the doctor, a genetic specialist, looked at the images and then turned to the Campbells. "I'm very sorry to tell you this, but there is something very wrong with your baby." He went on to explain that the sac of fluid showing at the base of their baby's neck indicated a 98 percent probability of a genetic defect. The doctor pulled out a chart, ran his finger down to the appropriate column, and read the stats. Sixty percent of babies with a similar buildup of fluid don't make it to twenty weeks, seventy-five percent of those who reach twenty weeks are not born alive, and of those who are, ninety-nine don't make it to their first

birthday. Without missing a beat, the doctor continued, "We can refer you to someone who can counsel you regarding this genetic information and refer you to someone to help you with next steps." When Christopher and Nancy asked what he meant by "next steps," the doctor said, "I would consider terminating the pregnancy given these initial findings."

Once the diagnosis of Trisomy 18 was confirmed, Christopher and Nancy never heard the word "baby" from their doctors again. They met Christopher and Nancy's refusal to abort with an escalating rhetoric of fear. The physicians they had trusted to deliver their baby turned against them and said that their pregnancy was "incompatible with life," would ruin their marriage and family, and was a "useless, wasted pregnancy." As their pastor, I remember those difficult early days of comforting Christopher and Nancy, astonished at how insensitive Nancy's ob-gyn acted in response to their decision to carry their baby.

The realization that they may never meet their baby hit Christopher and Nancy hard, and they began to grieve. It was so emotionally overwhelming for Nancy that it was difficult for her to pray. Christopher held her while she sobbed and prayed over her. Recalling those difficult moments, Nancy said, "It felt as though God was holding us." Judah, their bright two-and-a-half-year-old son, wanted to know, "Why is Mommy so sad?"

Help finally came to the Campbells through a "random" phone call from Mary, a genetic counselor connected to the lab that processed Nancy's blood work. When Nancy explained that she was not terminating her pregnancy, Mary didn't push back like the other doctors. Instead, she offered to help. Christopher conferenced in from work, and the two of them learned for the first time that they were having a girl. "Have you thought of any names?" the counselor asked. "We are going to call her Nora," Nancy replied. Then Mary offered to refer them to Children's Hospital of Philadelphia (CHOP), the hospital that would take over "Nora's" care.

Soon Christopher and Nancy were receiving expert care by some of the top neonatal specialists in the country. They were accepted by CHOP into their Garbose Family Special Delivery Unit, the world's "first birthing unit within a pediatric hospital dedicated to healthy mothers carrying babies with serious and life-threatening birth defects."[8] From that point on, Nora was never referred to as a fetus again and she had a team of doctors dedicated to her care.

Nancy and Nora received regular ultrasounds at CHOP by a top pediatric fetal geneticist. Their doctor, noticing that Nora's hands were formed with her index fingers pointing out, laughed and started calling her Annie Oakley, saying "She's got her guns out again." The 3D ultrasounds became the way Christopher and Nancy got to know their daughter.

As their delivery date approached and end-of-life decisions were laid out before them, Christopher and Nancy leaned upon the Lord for wisdom like never before. "As an engineer," Christopher said, "I could fix everything in my life, but I realized with Nora, there was nothing I could do to fix this. God taught me how much I really did not trust God and how self-reliant I lived day to day."

Nancy knew that God answered their prayers to allow Nora to survive her birth when, a few minutes into an emergency C-section, Nancy heard Nora cry. The nurses allowed Christopher to hold his daughter while they assessed her. One of the nurses took pictures for the Campbells. As the minutes passed, Nora became more quiet. At the end of the assessment, the neonatologist shook her head as Christopher handed Nora to Nancy and said, "There is nothing we can do." Reflecting on those moments, Christopher said, "We didn't have any decisions to make. God took control of the situation and made it clear that Nora's life was ending soon. She never opened her eyes, but she held my finger."

---

8   Children's Hospital of Philadelphia, "About the Garbose Family Special Delivery Unit," http://www.chop.edu/centers-programs/garbose-family-special-delivery-unit/about.

Nora didn't struggle. She quietly settled on Nancy's chest, breathing slowly as Nancy held her. Nancy recalled Nora's final moments saying, "Her heart rate continued to slow. We watched her quietly go. We told her we loved her, prayed with her, and we both kissed her goodbye."

By this time, I had arrived at the hospital and waited with the grandparents to meet Nora. When my turn came, an hour or so after her birth, she had already passed. I had to agree with everyone's assessment. Nora was beautiful.

As an extension of honoring life, the staff in the Special Delivery Unit understood dignity in death and the importance of giving parents the opportunity to grieve the loss of their child. They allowed the Campbells to keep Nora in Nancy's room. Any time the CHOP staff entered, from the top doctors down to the kitchen staff, they would express their sorrow and ask if they could greet Nora and report to the Campbells how beautiful she was.

The CHOP staff took plaster casts of Nora's feet. They welcomed Nora's brother, Judah, and allowed him to paint with his sister, as they moved her lifeless arms to create a memory for her older brother. They used an ink pad to make prints of Nora's hands and feet. Christopher and Nancy placed her handprint on two verses. Psalm 139 and Revelation 21. Christopher said, "The two verses encapsulated our thoughts, that God knit Nora together in Nancy's womb and one day, God will restore the creation and fix all Nora's problems."

"I think Revelation 21 never seemed so beautiful than in that moment," Christopher shared. "Up until that day, the earth seemed quite comfortable to me. Now the earth seems a lot paler and has lost its shine. Now we long for heaven. All of life's trials are because the world is fundamentally broken. The hope we hold is that one day he will make all things new." Nancy added, "Not just the erasing of our sorrow, but the joy that will come from being reunited with her." Today, when someone asks Judah how many siblings he has, he will say, "I have two. One that is dead, but that is okay, she lives in heaven and is joyful and safe. And I have one who lives on earth."

When it was time to say goodbye to Nora, the day of Nancy's discharge, the staff of the Special Delivery Unit gave the Campbells a memory box filled with her mementos. Every year the Campbells are welcomed back to the hospital around Christmastime, along with all the parents who have lost children at the unit, for a candlelight service and slideshow. Afterwards, the staff creates a yearbook with the photos of the slideshow and letters from the parents to their children. Christopher said, "God never lost sight of Nora, and he sent 'random' people to care for her. God never left our tomorrow to chance."

10. How did God use Nora's life for his good purposes?

11. How does remembering we will live forever affect the way we view stories like Nora's? How might it change your approach to parenting?

Respond

Spend time in group prayer. Pray for one participant's situation, and for other items springing from this week's study.

Before you leave, plan to take one or more of these *action steps* during the coming week. At the next study session, you'll have a chance to report on how it went.

- Read through the rest of Revelation 21. Imagine what it will be like when all our trials are over. Now imagine being there with all of your children. While our faith is weak at times to believe that some of them will ever get to heaven, we need to remember that "the arm of the LORD is not too short to save" (Isaiah 59:1 NIV). God is able to rescue the most rebellious of our kids.
- Personalize the words of the Lord's Prayer to fit your situation and then use it to pray to God for your needs. For example, "Let your kingdom come in the situation with _____. Let your will be done in _____'s life."
- What Scripture illustrating God's mercy can keep you anchored in Christ, avoiding bitterness when your children rebel? If you can't think of any, do an internet search for the top ten verses on the mercy of God. Choose a few to memorize.

Remember

Memorize Isaiah 59:1. "Surely the arm of the LORD is not too short to save, nor his ear too dull to hear" (NIV).

A GROWING PARENT

Main Idea

God uses our trials for our good, and through them helps us develop patience, compassion, and love.

To Prepare for Your Study Session

WEEK ONE

Read

Consider 1 Peter 1:3–12 by reading the devotions in chapter 13 of *Parenting First Aid*.

Review

We tend to think trials are bad, but God uses our trials for our good. While nobody wants to run out of gas, or suffer a flat tire, God can use these trials to build our faith. How many folks have been stranded on a rural road, then prayed to God for help, and had someone pull over to offer assistance?

The same is true of our family trials. I thought I was a patient man until I tried to potty-train our first son. He wouldn't have any part of it. God uses our parenting trials to teach us sacrificial love, longsuffering and endurance, and how to be slow to anger.

First Peter teaches us that God is using our trials to refine us like gold refined in a furnace. We complain about struggles because we forget about God and are caught up with the here and now. Our sovereign God stands over our trials, measuring them out perfectly for our growth. He sees eternity and knows how the trials he brings us today produce an eternal weight of glory (2 Corinthians 4:17).

Reflect

Answer the questions below as you read through chapter 13, or at the end of the week. Write out your answers and be ready to refer to them when your study session meets.

1. How can putting your present parenting trials in perspective against an eternity of trial-free life with Jesus give you strength and faith to endure today?

2. Second Corinthians 4:16–18 says, "Though our outer self is wasting away, our inner self is being renewed day by day. For this light momentary affliction is preparing for us an eternal weight of glory beyond all comparison, as we look not to the things that are seen but to the things that are unseen. For the things that are seen are transient, but the things that are unseen are eternal." Compare this to the message of 1 Peter 1:3–12. What are some parenting moments these passages speak to, and how do they encourage you?

3. How is God "renewing your inner self day by day" through your trials? What areas of sin is he seeking to remove? What grace is he interested in adding to your character? (Rather than fight against this process, welcome it in prayer before God.)

WEEK TWO

Read

Meditate on Psalm 103 as you read through chapter 14 in *Parenting First Aid* during week two.

Review

Psalm 103 is a one of those psalms you could read daily and never run out of depth for watering your soul. It contains God's description of himself that he first gave Moses in Exodus 34 when God hid him in the cleft of the rock and allowed him to see the back parts of his glory. While Moses received a privilege that we must wait to experience once in heaven—seeing God's glory with our eyes—the definition preserved in Psalm 103 is no less glorious. God wants to help us demonstrate the same glorious character in our families: that of one who is merciful and gracious, slow to anger and abounding in love.

When our children lash out against us with angry words and we respond with a gentle answer, we demonstrate the love of God. When our children mess up the same way for the fifteenth time and we respond by encouraging them instead of bringing judgment, we demonstrate the mercy of God. When our children are caught in their sin and we hold back the hammer of justice and instead offer them a kind reply, we demonstrate the mercy of God. One of the greatest opportunities we have in raising a family is demonstrating the loving-kindness of our God to our children.

Reflect

As you read through chapter 14, answer these questions to prepare for your study session.

4. Select a parenting concern from the list below and tell how Psalm 103 can encourage you in that situation.

   • When you see your children suffer
   • When you realize that your sin undermines your parenting
   • When sharing the gospel seems to have no effect on your kids
   • Other: _____

5. How well have you been modeling God's loving-kindness to your children? Where do you most need to grow?

6. Review Hebrews 12:3–12. What is the difference between the punishment of God for our sin and the loving discipline of the Lord? Why is it important to keep the Hebrews 12 passage in mind when you read Psalm 103?

7. How does remembering the cross add weight to the words, "So great is his steadfast love toward those who fear him" (Psalm 103:11)? How can the truth of verse 10, "He does not deal with us according to our sins, nor repay us according to our iniquities," motivate you to model this same love to your kids?

Study Session

Begin this session by reviewing the action steps from the end of the last study. Which steps did you take? What did you learn, or how were you encouraged?

Now go through the reflection questions for this study that you answered during the past few weeks. Pick some of them to discuss, or let each participant share the answers that were most meaningful to them. Then continue with the rest of this study.

Refuel

Psalm 17 is a prayer David wrote in the midst of one of his difficult trials. David's life was filled with trials: His father regarded his brothers as more important. When God raised him up to be king, Saul tried to kill him. David's own son rose up, rebelled against his father, and tried to take his throne.

Through his trials David learned to trust in God and not take things into his own hands. Let's allow Psalm 17 to help us trust God in two ways: (1) by letting go, knowing we are not in control of all things, and (2) by pressing in, knowing God is able to deliver us.

Hear a just cause, O Lord; attend to my cry!
Give ear to my prayer from lips free of deceit!
From your presence let my vindication come!

Let your eyes behold the right!
You have tried my heart, you have visited me by night,
    you have tested me, and you will find nothing;
    I have purposed that my mouth will not transgress.
With regard to the works of man, by the word of your lips
    I have avoided the ways of the violent.
My steps have held fast to your paths;
    my feet have not slipped.
I call upon you, for you will answer me, O God;
    incline your ear to me; hear my words.
Wondrously show your steadfast love,
    O Savior of those who seek refuge
    from their adversaries at your right hand. (Psalm 17:1–7)

8. Match one of your parenting concerns with a part of David's prayer in Psalm 17. How does the psalm encourage you?

9. Which of the things David prays most challenges you as a parent?

Relate

I can remember the day Lindsay handed me the legacy journal her father filled out for her. I knew as I received the book that she was entrusting me with an invaluable treasure. The contents of the pages revealed the thoughts of a man who desperately loved his daughters.

Though I am certain the sin he demonstrated in his early parenting years was great, the reflections I read in the pages of that journal reflected the thoughts of a man who finished well. He loved the Lord and wanted his daughters to follow after him.

God would use this journal to reach Lindsay and her sister Kelsey. Her father's love for Christ as written in its pages would compel Lindsay to open the Bible he left her and there she found salvation. Then Lindsay's prayers for Kelsey led to an accepted breakfast invitation to one of our Bridge evangelistic Bible studies, which led to her salvation. Read the story below, which comes from page 176 in *Parenting First Aid*, and discuss the questions.

> Lindsay and Kelsey grew up in a Christian home, surrounded by their mom's strong faith, though their father Jack didn't become a Christian until they were out of grade school. For most of their upbringing, he struggled with alcoholism. But once God opened his eyes to the truth of the gospel, Jack repented of his sin and his life dramatically changed. He stopped drinking and began to read the Bible, which Kelsey and Lindsay saw him study frequently. It seemed to them that he always had his Bible open. One of Jack's greatest desires was that his two daughters would turn from their sin and trust in Jesus.
>
> Lindsay, who called herself a Christian, didn't follow the Lord at that point. But she loved her dad very much and purchased a legacy journal at the local gift shop as a birthday present for him. The journal was designed for fathers to write out their life story for their children. Jack saw it as an opportunity to pass the gospel to his daughters. He cherished the gift and took seriously the task of answering the pages of questions. He returned the completed journal to Lindsay a year later. He finished the journal by writing a note to the girls on the extra blank pages.
>
> Lindsay and Kelsey,
>
> I've been through a lot in my life. Some good and some bad. You learn a lot as you are growing up and

you will make some mistakes. My prayer for the two of you is that you put your faith, love, and trust in the Lord Jesus Christ and pray and follow what he has in mind for you as you become young adults. I've asked the Lord so often to watch over you, and one day I won't be here any longer to help with that. I thank God for both of you every day and Lord willing, I'll be around for a while to watch you grow in Christ. Let our Lord Jesus Christ guide you through every day, and I hope you'll always love me as much as I love you!

Always! Dad

Jack didn't live long enough to see God answer his prayers for Lindsay and Kelsey's salvation. Cirrhosis and liver cancer, remnants of his former alcoholism, cut his life short. He died three years after returning the journal. Jack gave his two daughters another gift. On his deathbed, he called them to his side, handed Lindsay his Bible and said, "Please take this. I want you and Kelsey to read it."

In the months and years after her father's passing, Lindsay missed her dad. The journal he completed for her and her sister became a precious treasure, which she regularly turned to for comfort. It felt like she was spending time with him as she sat on her bed reading his answers to the many questions. As she read and reread the journal, she noticed that her dad kept talking about Jesus. She remembered the Bible he gave them and began to read it too. Reading his Bible cultivated an increasing hunger in her to know God like her dad knew God.

Eventually, the Spirit of God convicted Lindsay. She realized that she had to turn from her sin and live for Jesus. The day she decided to repent and trust Jesus, she felt a burden lift from her shoulders. Something had changed. Suddenly the pages of the journal sprang to life. Lindsay, recalling that moment shared, "I remember reading the pages in the journal after God saved me thinking—'Oh my goodness, I can't believe this. I'm feeling what Dad felt. Now I know what it feels like to know Jesus!'"

From that point on, Lindsay began to pray that God would save Kelsey and allow her to enjoy the freedom and joy she experienced. Kelsey was tangled in an unhealthy relationship with a guy and had pulled away from the family over the previous few years. So the phone call that came the night Lindsay prayed with Destin, Maria, and Emma was a miracle.

When Lindsay picked up Kelsey the next morning, Kelsey agreed to attend the breakfast at the church. Then she decided to stay for the message and discussion that followed. She was assigned to a small group that Destin and Lindsay helped lead. The breakfast and discussion seemed to go well, but when Lindsay asked Kelsey how she thought it went, Kelsey responded, "I probably won't come back." But inside God was working. She had enjoyed the message, which began to sink in over the following days. Kelsey's life was a mess and she felt broken. Though she lived an hour away and had to close her restaurant the night before the next Bridge meeting, she still was at the church when Lindsay arrived the next week. When Lindsay saw her sister's car, she began to rejoice.

A few weeks later, God began to close the deal on bringing Kelsey into his kingdom. One Bridge Course morning, Kelsey awoke with a start from a dream in which she was in a dark room, then turned a corner and saw Jesus hanging on the cross, crying out in agony. The message that day was on the crucifixion. It deeply affected Kelsey. She knew that the dream and the message came from God. "He wanted me to know it was real," she recalled. Finally, at week seven, Jack's prayers were answered as his second daughter called out to Jesus to forgive her sins. At that moment, like her sister, she felt a weight lift from her shoulders and knew that God had come into her life.

Immediately Kelsey's life began to change. She stopped drinking and smoking and started living for the Lord. Her boyfriend broke up with her, leaving her homeless, but her grandmother welcomed her into her home. Kelsey finished the Bridge Course, became a member of the church, and now prays for others who still need Jesus. While Jack's prayers for his daughters were not answered in his lifetime, they were answered nonetheless. Jesus said that there is great rejoicing in heaven whenever a sinner repents (Luke 15:7). Jack was present with Jesus in heaven when the Lord announced each daughter's salvation. We can be sure that no one cheered louder.

One of the questions in the journal Lindsay gave her father was, "What spiritual legacy would you like to leave for others?" Jack answered, "It comes from the Bible, James 1:12. 'Blessed is the man who perseveres under trial, because when he has stood the test, he will receive the crown of life that God has promised to those who love him'" (NIV). Lindsay and Kelsey are the two largest jewels that adorn Jack's crown. Today his daughters treasure the journal he wrote and long for the day when they are united with their dad and can thank him face to face.

10. How does this story encourage you to trust God for the salvation of your children?

11. How might writing reach your children in ways conversations may fall short?

Respond

Spend time in group prayer. Pray for one participant's situation, and for other items springing from this week's study.

Before you leave, plan to take one or more of these *action steps* during the coming week. At the next study session, you'll have a chance to report on how it went.

- Write out a prayer that asks God to help you in your trials but also asks the Lord to increase your longing for heaven and a day when your present trials are over.

- Call out to the Lord, personalizing 1 Peter 1:8–9 to tell the Lord of your love for him. It is a holy thing for us to praise God as we endure our trials and to celebrate his goodness even while we struggle through doubts.
- Have you ever noticed that when we focus on our troubles it means we first took our eyes off God? Make a list of all your troubles, then fold it up and put it aside. Read through Psalm 103 aloud. Speak the words of the psalm aloud and up to the heavens as your prayer. Then ask God to renew your faith and strength, and to take the burden of your troubles away.

Remember

Memorize 2 Corinthians 4:17. "For this light momentary affliction is preparing for us an eternal weight of glory beyond all comparison."

A GOSPEL-TELLING PARENT

Main Idea

The gospel story of God's deliverance is a gift we must pass on to our children.

To Prepare for Your Study Session

WEEK ONE

Read

Read chapter 15 in *Parenting First Aid*, which looks at Exodus 10:1–15.

Review

All of Scripture tells the story of deliverance from the curse of sin. Immediately after the fall of Adam and Eve in the book of Genesis, the drama and suspense of God's story of redemption begins. Eve would bear a son who would one day crush the head of the serpent, a sign that the curse of sin would be reversed. From there, the suspense and excitement build. Is God's promised deliverer Abel? Is it Noah and his ark? Is it Joseph, saving Israel from the famine?

By the book of Exodus, when Moses is chosen by God to deliver his people from Egypt, the story has taken some amazing twists. Instead of leading his people out of Egypt with one sweeping victory, God creates a drawn-out drama of ten plagues. God uses these plagues to display his power and authority to Pharaoh, but he hardens Pharaoh's heart so that he will not let God's people go. God does this, he tells us in chapter 10, to create a story for the parents of Israel to tell their future children, so that they might believe. God wrote this drama, which climaxes with the coming of Jesus and his resurrection from the dead, to reach our children. He wrote this story to help you reach your kids.

As we recount the story to our children, they get to see the almighty hand of God deliver his people. Through it they see God's power, but more importantly they come to know his character—his unfailing love, forgiveness, and mercy toward a people who sin again and again. As parents, we need to trust in God's plan and put our faith for our children's salvation in the power of God's Word, not in the skill of our parenting.

Reflect

Answer these questions as you read through chapter 15 in *Parenting First Aid*, or when you finish. Write your answers down so you can discuss some answers later, if you want, with your group.

1. Think of some Bible stories or passages that have special meaning to you. How might you share that meaning with your children? Think also of how God has been faithful to you or your family. Which of these stories do your kids need to hear?

2. Read Exodus 3:7–10. How can God's hearing of Israel's cries for deliverance encourage us to continue praying for our children?

3. In John 6:37–39, Jesus says, "All that the Father gives me will come to me, and whoever comes to me I will never cast out. For I have come down from heaven, not to do my own will but the will of him who sent me. And this is the will of him who sent me, that I should lose nothing of all that he has given me, but raise it up on the last day." How does this continue the theme that God will not leave behind a single one of his children?

4. How can knowing God's commitment to deliver his people encourage your faith regarding your children?

WEEK TWO

Read

Reflect on Proverbs 3:1–8 as you read through chapter 16 of *Parenting First Aid*.

Review

Solomon wrote proverbs for his sons to help them walk through the trials of life they were sure to face. He assured them that if they remembered his teaching it would adorn them like a string of pearls (Proverbs 1:9), help them know God (Proverbs 2:5), and help them find peace (Proverbs 3:2).

All of Proverbs can be summarized with one simple verse: "Trust in the LORD with all your heart, and do not lean on your own understanding" (Proverbs 3:5). These sixteen words, which are easy to comprehend, are impossible to accomplish without God's help. The words of the verse are easy to say, but tough to follow. But if we cry out to God and ask for his help to apply this verse to our lives, the promise of peace we read in chapter two is ours for the taking.

Parenting gives us daily opportunities to realize we need to trust God and can't lean on our own understanding. The bottom line: we simply do not have what it takes to go it alone. The good news is that God promises that if we place our trust in him for our kids, he will make our paths straight. This doesn't mean we won't have our ups and downs, but God will be with us and day by day we make it through. Yesterday's grace is not sufficient to carry us through the next, but the knowledge that God kept us yesterday, and the day before, and the day before that, helps us to trust him and make it through our tomorrows.

Reflect

Think about these questions based on chapter 16 of *Parenting First Aid*, and write down your answers.

5. How have you found yourself feeling hopeless or complaining to God that he hasn't delivered you, instead of continuing to ask for his deliverance?

6. How confident are you that, if you were to follow God's commands, you would find peace in the midst of your parenting storms? What does your answer tell you about your level of faith in God?

7. Proverbs 3:5 begins with the phrase, "Trust in the LORD." What might trusting in the Lord look like in a normal day of interacting with your children? Give an example.

8. Can you remember a time when you put your trust in the Lord and found peace in the midst of a parenting storm? Tell about it. (Remembering what God has done in the past is one of the most effective ways to trust God in the present. Like the Israelites, we too often forget our past deliverance amid present storms.)

Study Session

Begin this session by reviewing the action steps from the end of the last study. Which steps did you take? What did you learn, or how were you encouraged?

Now go through the reflection questions for this study that you answered during the past few weeks. Pick some of them to discuss, or let each participant share the answers that were most meaningful to them. Then continue with the rest of this study.

Refuel

God gave Solomon great wisdom, and Solomon used that gift to write simple truths to guide our lives. By following Solomon's proverbs, we get to share in his amazing wisdom. And because the Holy Spirit inspired his words, we can be certain they are true.

It is easy to doubt that God hears our prayers while we are enduring a persistent trial, one where we cry out night and day with no answer to show for our prayers. Solomon assures us in Proverbs 15:29 that God hears us. For those who are in Christ, we need not be afraid that our wickedness might cause God to refuse us, for in Christ we stand righteous before him. "For our sake he made him to be sin who knew no sin, so that in him we might become the righteousness of God" (2 Corinthians 5:21).

> The LORD is far from the wicked, but he hears the prayer of the righteous. (Proverbs 15:29)

9. What is different about your prayer life when you pray with the assurance that God sees you as righteous?

10. How should Proverbs 15:29 affect the way you pray for yourself and your children, or how might it change what you pray for?

Relate

As I am writing this study guide, I realize that a new generation has come into my life since first writing *Parenting First Aid*. The floor of our living room is once again scattered with toddler toys. My daughter's son, Zion, is a regular over at our house, and he has a younger sister on the way with the name Hosanna awaiting her arrival.

Lois and I are hard at work again trusting God, this time for our grandchildren. Once again, we will get the opportunity to tell them the wonderful story of God's gospel deliverance. We'll tell them the story of the Exodus, and the life and crucifixion of Jesus. Then we'll tell the story of how God saved their mom and dad. Then, by God's grace we will watch as God uses the trials of their lives to bring them to Christ. Read the story (reprinted from page 192 of *Parenting First Aid*) and discuss the questions.

I can remember holding my newborn daughter Emma in my arms, comforting her late-night crying and wondering about her future. Who would she grow up to be? How would God save her? Whom would she marry? As I sang lullabies to comfort her crying, I prayed God would rescue her from sin and guide her. God answered my prayers. Emma grew up to be a fine, godly, respectful daughter. God drew her to himself in her early high school years. She studied elementary education and pursued a missional teaching position in the impoverished inner city, which wasn't a part of my comfortably fabricated future for her.

As for marriage, well, let's say God wasn't following my comfortable script for that either. I'll never forget the day Emma pulled Lois and me aside in the kitchen to talk. She and Martha had reached out to Destin after he returned home to recover from his gunshot wound. Each Sunday night they, along with my son Noah, hung out around a bonfire with a group of older teens and college students to worship, pray, and fellowship. It was there that Emma noticed God touching Destin's life.

After pulling us aside, Emma said, "I believe God wants me to pray for Destin because he is going to become my husband. What is up with that?" She went on to explain her concerns given his addictive past, his need to be established in a career, and the fact that it would be years before he would be able to marry. She was torn. She could see God at work in his life, but the obstacles to a future together weighed on the other side of the balance scale like a cinderblock.

My mind raced as she spoke. Only a few weeks earlier, Destin had scheduled a pastoral appointment to meet with me. Even though I had cared for his family for many years, I was aware that twenty-something guys didn't schedule appointments with me unless they were interested in one of my daughters—which he was. Destin began our meeting by confessing his sin and bringing me up to date on his failures. He wouldn't be ready to pursue a wife until he was clean for a year, he explained. Destin needed to pay off his mountain of fines, get a job, and establish a career so that he could provide before he would be ready to marry. But, he added, he was interested in my daughter.

I didn't dare let on to Emma or Lois anything about the earlier conversation. I just listened and prayed for wisdom. I agreed with Emma that Destin was in no place to pursue a relationship, but for now she should at least follow the impression to pray for him. Inside, God began working on my heart and impressed the question upon me: *Do you believe in redemption?* For years, I counseled Destin's mother, Maria, encouraging her that God could save her son and deliver him from drugs. Now that it was happening, was I willing to allow God to use my daughter as a part of his restoration plan?

As the months unfolded, Destin continued pressing into God and reaching others caught in the prison of drug addiction. The bonfire crowd prayed fervently for their friends, and young men and women were getting saved. They started sitting in the front row of our church on Sunday, lifting their hands, praising God for his deliverance, with my daughter Emma smack in the middle of them.

Destin, who had always had an incredible work ethic, took a job with his uncle installing garage doors. He soon ran installations without supervision. He began paying off all his debts, stayed clean and, most importantly, demonstrated a passion for God that affected everyone around him. Six months later he was back in my office to give me an update and share his desire to pursue my daughter Emma.

I reminded him of the wisdom of waiting a year, but inside I was concerned that this wouldn't be nearly enough time. I could not deny God's work in Destin's life, but I found it difficult to add my daughter into the equation of God's redemption. In the meantime, Emma grew in her affection for Destin as she prayed for him. We directed her to seek God further and helped her count the costs of pursuing a relationship with a man with his past.

A year from our first November meeting, Destin's name appeared in my pastoral schedule again. I knew he had remained drug-free and paid off his debt. He continued to minister to others who were now getting baptized and joining our church. The fruit of God's grace on Destin's life was evident for all to see. In that meeting, Destin asked for permission to pursue my daughter. I agreed.

A few weeks later, Emma shared with Destin the prayer journal entry she had written years before, when she began to pray for her future husband's salvation. Destin was amazed to discover that the very week she started her journal was the same week he knelt in his prison cell and gave his life to Christ, after a phone call with his mom.

Within a few months, Destin was back in my office, asking to marry my daughter. Things were going far too fast for my comfort. He explained that he believed God was bringing the two of them together and referenced the timing of Emma's journal and his salvation.

Then Destin pulled out a piece of paper and began to read a list of vows—but not vows he planned to vow to Emma. This was a list of vows to me, her father. As he read each one carefully and looked into my eyes, vowing to care for my daughter, the Spirit of God filled my heart. As he spoke, I could not deny the miracle God had accomplished in his life. Destin explained that he paid off his fines and debt, and established a career, excelling at his work. And, to my shock, he already had a ring.

He stuck his hand in his pocket and pulled out a diamond engagement ring of inestimable value, for it was the ring his father had given his mother, Maria. I knew the moment I saw the ring that God was doing a miracle before my eyes. Then Destin read to me the letter his mother had presented with the ring.

Dear Destin,

I am full of joy with the work the Father has done and is doing in your life, and I am so pleased with how you have chosen Emma, a beautiful, godly woman, to be by your side and walk through life and ministry with.

This ring is a symbol of eighteen years of faithful marriage between me and your dad. Your father was a man of faith who loved God first, then his wife with all his heart. He cared for, protected, and provided for his family with vigilance. This ring reminds me of his steadfast love for me, as Christ loved the church. I trust that you will be the same for Emma.

Consider this ring, the ring that your dad pledged his love to me, as "the crown with which his mother crowned him on the day of his wedding, on the day of the gladness of his heart" (Song of Songs 3:11).

I am rejoicing with you as I know your father is too, and I pass down this ring to you with all my love and blessing. Mom

At that moment, I had a choice to make. Did I truly believe in God's deliverance? That question swirled in my mind, quickly followed by the answer I gave Destin as he asked for my daughter's hand. "Yes," I told him.

While the Enemy means to imprison our children in bondage to sin, God is about writing a story of deliverance. He hears our prayers and calls for mercy, and we must not give up praying, knowing that he can deliver our children and weave them into his grand tapestry of grace. We will celebrate the testimony of his grace for all time and eternity as we each, in turn, share story after story of God's redeeming work.

Lois and I met at Maria's house after the engagement to celebrate. Maria smiled as we considered all that God had done. It was truly remarkable. Reflecting on the many years I had encouraged her to stay the course and trust God and his redemption, Maria said, "Who would have known or believed that your daughter Emma was a part of the plan?"

11. How are you encouraged by how God brought Destin, a heroin addict, together with Emma, a woman who loved the Lord?

12. Think of a time in your life when you saw God at work writing your story and conforming your life to his wonderful plan. Tell about it.

Respond

Spend time in group prayer. Pray for one participant's situation, and for other items springing from this week's study.

Before you leave, plan to take one or more of these *action steps* during the coming week. At the next study session, you'll have a chance to report on how it went.

• Write out a prayer that declares, before God and all the forces of evil, your renewed commitment to insist that all your children go with you to the Promised Land. Ask God to deliver them from

Egypt, a picture of the wicked bondage of sin and the flesh. Pray this prayer the rest of the week.

- Look up the following Scriptures: John 3:16; Isaiah 44:3–5; Isaiah 54:13–14; Acts 16:31. How do these passages point to God's commitment to save every one of his children?

- Make a list of the past times that you trusted God in a trial and found peace. Then reflect on the unchangeable nature of God. He is the same God today, who still offers his steadfast love and peace for our present trials.

Remember

Memorize Proverbs 3:5–6. "Trust in the LORD with all your heart, and do not lean on your own understanding. In all your ways acknowledge him, and he will make straight your paths."

AN ENDURING PARENT

Main Idea

Parenting is like a marathon, but God is there to run with us.

To Prepare for Your Study Session

WEEK ONE

Read

Read through chapter 17 in *Parenting First Aid*, which contains thoughts on Hebrews 12:1–4.

Review

To many new couples, parenting feels like a destination—something you long for and hope you will see one day. When that day arrives, as you hold your newborn baby in your hands you feel like you made it. But then a day or so later, when the nurse informs you that you are being discharged and asks, "Do you have a car seat?" you suddenly realize they are actually allowing you to take your son or daughter home. In that moment, and for the rest of your life, you realize that parenting is not a destination on a map; it is a continual state of living.

Hebrews 12 compares life as a believer to a runner in a race. And if you have children, you are a parent-runner. From the moment the judge offers his pronouncement in an adoption, or the doctor his congratulations that it's a baby boy or girl, you run the race as a mom or dad. The joys and thrills of parenting can provide a second wind when, in that race, trials blow against you. Parenting can also present its own list of hardships that threaten to steal our peace. It is critical that in those times we keep our eyes focused on Jesus, the founder and perfecter of our faith

Reflect

Answer these questions along with your chapter 17 reading. Write down your answers so you have them for the study session.

1. How can remembering all that Jesus suffered help you endure one of your particular parenting trials?

2. How is God using your parenting trials to grow and refine you? Consider some items from the list and describe your experience.

   • A habit of faith I've learned, through trials, to practice

   • A sin I've learned, through trials, to repent of

- A parenting "idol" I've learned, through trials, to let go of

- A self-sufficiency I've learned, through trials, to trust God for

- A strength I've learned, through trials, to become humble about

- A godly duty I've learned, through trials, to embrace

- Other (explain)

3. Page 217 of *Parenting First Aid* mentions how we can't discipline our teens as though they are still toddlers. Are there any areas in which you are trying to discipline your teens like toddlers? If so, what struggles might the Lord want you to release back to him?

WEEK TWO

Read

During your second week, prepare by reading about John 17:1–26 in chapter 18 of *Parenting First Aid*.

Review

While most Christians believe that God speaks to us through the Scriptures that he first gave to others, the places where God speaks directly to the future generations carry a special encouragement. John 17 contains one of these encouraging verses. There, in the midst of a prayer for the disciples, Jesus extends his prayer to you and me.

John 17 becomes even more helpful when we realize that Jesus, two thousand years ago, knew as he prayed that you would be a mom or dad. So his prayer for you includes his understanding of your circumstances as a parent. Once you understand that, John 17 works to anchor you through your parenting storms. How encouraging it is to know that Jesus prayed that his Father would protect you from the evil one and sanctify you with his truth! By this prayer we know that God will help us when the enemy throws his fiery darts against us and when the evil of this world assaults our family. You can be sure God the Father heard and will answer his Son's prayer to keep you and preserve you. Knowing Jesus is interceding for you can help you as you run the parenting marathon.

Reflect

Answer the following questions as part of your reading of chapter 18 in *Parenting First Aid*. Be ready to share some of your answers, if you want, when your study session meets.

4. How should knowing that Jesus is at the right hand of the Father, interceding for you, affect the way you pray for your children and for your parenting?

5. What can you learn about the Father's character from the way Jesus lifted up his requests to him?

6. How can the confidence Jesus had when he prayed for his disciples encourage you in your prayers for your children?

Study Session

Begin this session by reviewing the action steps from the end of the last study. Which steps did you take? What did you learn, or how were you encouraged?

Now go through the reflection questions for this study that you answered during the past few weeks. Pick some of them to discuss, or let each participant share the answers that were most meaningful to them. Then continue with the rest of this study.

Refuel

Jesus loves and cares about your children. During his earthly ministry, parents brought their children to Jesus so that he could pray for them (Matthew 19:13–15). When the disciples tried to chase the children away, thinking Jesus had more important things to do, Jesus rebuked them. He said, "Let the little children come to me and do not hinder them, for to such belongs the kingdom of heaven" (Matthew 19:14). Jesus has not changed. That is why we can have confidence as parents when we are bringing our prayers for our children to Jesus and asking for his help.

If Jesus were walking the earth today, wouldn't you want to bring your children to him and ask him to pray? Remember Jesus is in heaven interceding for you (Hebrews 7:25). So go with confidence in prayer and bring your children to Jesus who said, "Let the little children come."

7. If Jesus were with us on earth today, what would you ask him to do in your children's lives? You can offer that same request as a prayer up to heaven.

8. The disciples thought life was too busy with more important things than praying for children. How can your own busy schedule distract you from making time to bring your children to Jesus? What are some occasions when you could pray for them but usually don't?

Relate

Going through the teenage rebellion of our oldest son, Nathan, brought Lois and me to our knees in prayer. Looking back, it is easy to see how God designed the trial of our son's rebellion to discipline us and to teach us to trust more in God than in our own strength. I'm thankful that God surrounded us with wise counselors who helped us recognize the Lord's work through what felt like a marathon. They reminded us that God was after our hearts as much as our son's. At times, it felt as though it would never end, but God was wonderfully merciful. In his perfect time, he reached down and rescued our son.

Since then, God has used our story and Nathan's testimony to encourage hundreds of parents. Having shared some of the trials we faced during Nathan's rebellion, I wanted to give Nathan the opportunity to share the testimony of his rescue, which he was eager to do. Here is Nathan's story as he tells it, from page 218 in *Parenting First Aid*.

> I woke up, threw on a T-shirt and a fresh pair of jeans. It was the morning after Thanksgiving, and I knew it was going to be a fantastic day. I jumped into my car, sped down the road, and quickly arrived at a local shopping center, the usual meeting place for me and my buddies. As a young teen, I had built a reputation for questionable behavior and always needed a legitimate reason for my parents to let me go out with my friends. Today was perfect because I had a good excuse to get out of the house—Black Friday shopping. I was filled with excitement and felt like I could conquer the world.
>
> My friends and I piled into one vehicle and headed to the mall. After a long day of shopping and fun, we drove to the lot where we'd all parked. Once we were back at our cars, a friend pulled out a pipe of marijuana to smoke, which, unbeknownst to my parents, was something I had done with my friends before.
>
> But this day was different. Not long after we parked, we heard sirens. I turned toward the sound and, to my dismay, saw the terrifying gleam of red and blue lights right behind our car.

Looking back, I believe that God sent that police officer. My parents had warned me. They were praying I would get caught every time I strayed. Even though I wasn't ready to live for Christ and change my ways, God allowed me to feel the weight of my sin that day. Eventually, I realized my desperate need for a Savior.

It didn't take long for the police to discover what we were doing. Within minutes, all three of us were handcuffed, placed in different cop cars, and driven to the police station down the road. My heart was racing. All I could think about was my family. How I let them down. How they would never trust or forgive me again.

Throughout my teen years, I caused trouble for my parents. I purchased a cell phone behind their back that I had delivered to a post office box I rented to keep my parents from seeing what I got in the mail. I frequently snuck out of the house late at night and began dating a girl from work without telling them what was going on. The older I got, the more opportunities I found to disobey their rules. My parents would respond in the usual way. Dad would limit my freedom, trying to prevent me from making more bad choices. He would pray for me and read the Bible with me. Dad spent countless hours meeting with me, pointing me to Jesus and trying to understand what was going on in my life. Still, I would find ways to hide what I was doing and at times I would secretly mock his attempts to control my behavior.

As I sat in the holding cell waiting for Dad to pick me up, I expected that this time I'd get an angry response. He would most certainly ground me for months, possibly even the rest of my life. At the very least, I knew that I was going to get my phone and car taken away.

Once my dad arrived, the police released me. When we got in the car, he turned to me, looked me straight in the eye, and said "I love you, son. We all make mistakes, and I believe that God had you get caught today because he has a bigger plan for you in your life." He said, "This isn't the end of the road. It's the beginning."

I wish I could say that this gracious response made me immediately change my ways. It didn't. I needed God to do that. I continued to get in trouble and lie to my family. Mom and Dad kept responding with grace and love that I certainly did not deserve. When parents respond with love (instead of anger) toward their wayward son or daughter, it demonstrates the grace of God, who does not treat us as our sins deserve. Trust me, flipping out on your kids, though they may deserve it, doesn't help them draw near to God. But love, demonstrated through kindness, breaks down the emotional barriers teens build to shut out parental advice and direction. The love of Jesus portrayed through a gracious, forgiving response can be used by God to soften their hardened hearts and open their ears to hear God's voice.

Although I believed in God and considered myself a Christian, I lived for myself. My decisions revolved around doing what I thought would make me happy. As I tried to negotiate my parents' rules, my friends from church would often make jokes about how strict our parents were, and how boring it would be to follow everything the Bible taught. As a result, I couldn't see how living for God would be any fun because much of my joy came from worldly pleasures.

Still, my selfishness and lust for sin were taking a toll on my life and my relationships, especially with my girlfriend, Lauren. She loved me, but my sneaking around, lying, and getting into trouble wasn't exactly great leadership, and was hurting our relationship. Thankfully, God continued to allow me to get caught again and again. Finally, a more serious run-in with the law resulted in the suspension of my junior driver's license. I was stopped in my tracks—literally! God used that event and its consequences to show me how careless, reckless, and immature I had been. I knew that I needed to change, but I was afraid.

I went to my parents, asking for help and forgiveness. Mom and Dad, as they had been in every other instance, forgave me with open arms and an open heart and pointed me to God. I knew that the pleasure I was chasing wasn't going to fulfill me. By the grace of God, I gave up fighting on my own and put my trust in Jesus to help me defeat my sin. I had a sense of peace and the overwhelming feeling that the Holy Spirit was with me now and forever. In the past, I had always felt that I was living my life "on the fence," but now I could confidently say which side of the fence I was on. I was filled with hope that God had a plan to use my life to bring him glory. Those years were not wasted. God had used them to show me how much I needed his grace in my life.

Dad set aside specific times to meet with me on a more regular basis, and he pointed me toward Jesus by the use of his Word. As the father from the parable in Luke 15 welcomed back the prodigal son, so my dad welcomed me back. It took some time, but I was slowly able to mend the relationships I had broken in my years of sin and selfishness. Slowly, my family began to trust me again. My friends looked up to me and respected me. And that girlfriend, Lauren, became my wife in the fall of 2015.

Your children will disobey you, and some will test you to your core. But before you respond in anger, take a step back and breathe deeply. Pray for grace, help, and guidance in disciplining your son or daughter. The gracious responses my parents demonstrated toward me opened my eyes to God's love and mercy. God can help your kids realize that same truth.

9. How were you affected by reading Nathan's story?

10. What parenting examples, good or bad, can you learn from in this story, and what do you learn from those examples?

Respond

Spend time in group prayer. Pray for one participant's situation, and for other items springing from this week's study.

Before you leave, plan to take one or more of these *action steps* during the coming week. At the next study session, you'll have a chance to report on how it went.

- Where have you seen God at work, disciplining your older children through the trials of life? Look for an opportunity to share with your kids the ways you see God disciplining you as your loving Father. Let them know that as they get older, God in his kindness will discipline them too, for he chastises "every son whom he receives" (Hebrews 12:6).
- Call out to Jesus and ask him to fulfill in your children these prayers from the first portion of Jesus's High Priestly Prayer in John 17:1–18.
  - » That your children will come to know the truth of the gospel: that the Father sent his Son to die on the cross for our sins.
  - » That they would believe the gospel.
  - » That they would keep God's Word.
  - » That they would live in unity with other believers.

Remember

Memorize Nahum 1:7. "The Lord is good, a stronghold in the day of trouble; he knows those who take refuge in him."

A HOPEFUL PARENT

Main Idea

The resurrection of Jesus is the foundation for our hope and trust in God, for us and our children.

To Prepare for Your Study Session

WEEK ONE

Read

Study Psalm 16 by reading through chapter 19 in *Parenting First Aid*.

Review

Like it did for David, our confidence as we walk through life's difficulties comes from our trust in God. David's trust that God would hold him fast through his trials was rooted in his belief in God's unshakable plan. God spoke to David and promised to establish his house and his kingdom forever (2 Samuel 7:16). In Psalm 16, we get a glimpse of one of David's prayers and can see him wrestle with his faith. We ultimately watch as he trusts God for the trial he faced. God would not abandon David to the grave.

Beyond David, this psalm points to the resurrection of Jesus, a descendant of David. God the Father also would not abandon his Son Jesus to the grave. Jesus rose again and, as a result, David's trust in God's plan resulted in salvation for David. So too our trust in Jesus results in salvation for us. And it builds our confidence that God's promises apply to our lives, for we are his children.

When you add life's challenges together—financial concerns, work-related trials, health issues—and then mix in the daily challenges that come with parenting, it is easy to get overwhelmed. It is into this mix that we need to remember that our time in this life is short. While trials here may plague us for a season, they will not ultimately subdue us. One day, when the Lord returns or if he tarries and we pass into death, we wake up in victory with Jesus. Then we will say goodbye to all our trials forever. So, whether God answers our prayers and delivers us from our trials here in this life or we need to wait until the next, we will see victory, for God will not abandon us to the grave.

Reflect

The questions below accompany your reading of chapter 19 in *Parenting First Aid*. Write out your answers.

1. God uses parenting struggles to "shake away" our trust in things that do not last, so that we trust only in God and become parents who "shall not be shaken (Psalm 16:8). Which of your false trusts or sins do you think God is trying to shake away through the trials he designed for you?

2. When you see your parenting not only for what it means in this life, but also through the lens of an eternal kingdom, how does that change your perspective on your trials?

3. How can trusting in God's promises help you grow in your joy despite your trials?

4. When it comes to parenting, our confidence must be based on God, not in our own ability. Read through Psalm 16 again. Which verses reveal David placing his trust in God? Describe a typical parenting moment in your life when it would help to remember one of those verses.

WEEK TWO

Read

Read through chapter 20, about Ephesians 1:1–15, in *Parenting First Aid*.

Review

As Christian parents, we carry a burden for our children's salvation, but too often we allow that burden to morph into a responsibility. We mistakenly believe we are responsible to save our children. We confuse our responsibility to teach them the gospel with God's responsibility to change their hearts. Should a child rebel against us and God, we suffer under the weight of condemnation and blame ourselves for their failure.

Ephesians 1 sets the record straight. God is the author of salvation and it comes to all by his grace alone. If God determined the day of our child's salvation before the foundations of the world were laid, and he is going to work it by his grace, then it can't be our responsibility to save them. It must be God's job. We do have a responsibility to share the gospel and water the seed we plant with our prayers, but God alone determines the exact moment the scales of unbelief will fall from their eyes and he alone holds the keys to their deliverance from sin. Parents who try to shoulder God's responsibility are easily crushed under the weight of that burden. But when we realize the weight of our children's salvation is carried by God on his shoulders, and we come out from under the burden of that yoke, we can delight in the grace of God and experience the freedom from condemnation that comes from trusting God to do what only God can do.

Reflect

Now answer these questions that go with chapter 20 in *Parenting First Aid*.

5. Why do some believers find it easy to see God's grace for themselves and for other people's children, but hard to see how God could have grace for their own children?

6. How might you use Ephesians 1:1–15 to answer the accusation, "This child is too rebellious to be saved"?

7. Where have you seen God use evil to accomplish his good, working things to fulfill his master plan?

8. Where have you seen the Spirit of God at work in your life? What could you tell your children about what God is doing in your life?

Study Session

Begin this session by reviewing the action steps from the end of the last study. Which steps did you take? What did you learn, or how were you encouraged?

Now go through the reflection questions for this study that you answered during the past few weeks. Pick some of them to discuss, or let each participant share the answers that were most meaningful to them. Then continue with the rest of this study.

Refuel

Whenever we pray, it is important to have faith in God. Our faith is not in our faith, which is often frail and weak; our faith is in a faithful God who can and will answer our prayers. If we believe God is able, is willing, and works all things together for our good, then we can have faith that God will answer our prayers—according to his will and purpose and in his time.

God doesn't expect us to have perfect faith. When a man whose son was demon possessed asked Jesus to heal his son, Jesus replied, "All things are possible for one who believes." The father of the boy responded honestly, "I believe, help my unbelief" (Mark 9:23–24). What did Jesus do in response to this father's imperfect faith? Jesus healed his son. So, as you read through Mark 11:22–25 now, remember the prayer of that father whose story Mark recorded two chapters earlier. Jesus's call to have faith comes on the heels of evidence that even halting faith which needs much strengthening from God—indeed, faith as small as a single mustard seed (Luke 17:6)—will move the heart of God to action.

> And Jesus answered them, "Have faith in God. Truly, I say to you, whoever says to this mountain, 'Be taken up and thrown into the sea,' and does not doubt in his heart, but believes that what he says will come to pass, it will be done for him. Therefore I tell you, whatever you ask in prayer, believe that you have received it, and it will be yours. And whenever you stand praying, forgive, if you have anything against anyone, so that your Father also who is in heaven may forgive you your trespasses." (Mark 11:22–25)

9. How does this Scripture encourage you to pray with renewed faith for your children in one of the following parenting struggles?

- When your child seems uninterested in God
- When your child won't respond well to discipline
- When you realize your discipline is being undermined by your own anger, desire for control, withdrawal, or other sin
- When there's an illness or other danger
- When you find you have failed to teach, discipline, or provide for your child the way you should
- Other: _____

10. Why is it important to remember that your faith is in God, not in
    your measure of faith or the quality of your prayers?

Relate

As of the writing of this study guide, the Stanleys are still at it,
faithfully guiding their special-needs children through the many trials
life brings. Every Sunday, David walks into church like a shepherd,
watching over his little sheep Becky as she toggles her power wheelchair
through the door. She thinks she is in control, and to a point she is. But
Dad is never far behind, watching over her and helping her watch out
for us, so that we don't get bowled over. Becky is always eager to insist
David explain how his tie matches her dress. She doesn't use words, so I
can't understand her, but David knows just what she is communicating
and speaks first for Becky and then for him, answering her question or
explaining his tie. Somehow, when I watch his kind and patient love for
his daughter, I am strengthened to endure the smaller parenting trials I
face. Here is his story, from page 244 of *Parenting First Aid*.

> I first met David and Grace Stanley the hard way—over the
> phone, as the children's pastor, calling them to apologize. That
> Sunday, one of my workers had told David that their son Lang
> was no longer welcome in the classroom. Lang had been dis-
> ruptive, but we should have engaged his parents much differ-
> ently. By the time I found out, David and Grace were already
> gone. When I spoke with him over the phone, David graciously
> forgave me and agreed to give our ministry a second chance at
> caring for his son. Then he revealed a long history of rejection
> from churches because of their children's special needs.

Their calling to care for children in need began two months after they were married when, due to his mother's illness, David and Grace welcomed his younger brother and sister (five and eight years old) into their home, where they remained until adulthood. After adding four natural-born children to their clan, they answered a call to serve in a pilot foster day-care program. Their experience as part-time foster parents moved them to become full-time foster parents. Shortly thereafter, they added baby Grace to the Stanley family. Baby Grace lived with them for eighteen months. When they expressed an interest in adopting Grace, they were denied because of the color of their skin. Grace was then given up for adoption to another couple, leaving the Stanleys heartbroken.

That didn't stop the agency from placing another foster child in the Stanley home. Tina was diagnosed with a condition called "failure to thrive." Tina suffered from seizures and was profoundly mentally handicapped. Part of her brain never developed. David fought vigorously as her advocate in a health care system where foster children often slipped through the cracks. The Stanleys were moved by God's charge to Israel from Leviticus 19: "When a stranger sojourns with you in your land, you shall not do him wrong. You shall treat the stranger who sojourns with you as the native among you, and you shall love him as yourself, for you were strangers in the land of Egypt: I am the Lord your God" (Leviticus 19:33–34).

Even with the best of care, Tina never went beyond the developmental level of a six-month-old. She became their first adopted daughter and thrived in the love-saturated Stanley home until the Lord took her home to glory at age fifteen. When I asked David and Grace how they have remained unshaken through the devastating losses and challenges in caring for children like Tina, David said, "It is God's sovereignty that holds me. I believe he is in control of every detail of the universe and every detail of my life. 'And we know that for those who love God all things work together for good' (Romans 8:28). I may not always know how the circumstances of life will unfold, but I know they are there for my good. We are clay in the potter's hands, or like the dough my wife Grace pounds as she kneads it on the board. He is making us useful. God has a purpose. I might not see it now, but one day he will make it known. God gave us these children; how could we not take them in?"

Three years after taking in Tina, the Stanleys were asked to take in Niki, an infant with a tracheotomy. "Since Tina was easy," David shared, "we figured we could handle another child. After all, we thought, how hard could it be to care for a child with a trach?"

They soon found that it was hard, very hard. The day they received Niki, the medical staff told the Stanleys that she would likely have the trach in for five to seven years and said it was unlikely that she would ever be capable of much physical activity. "Don't be surprised if she doesn't make it through the night," one doctor warned. Niki made it through the night in spite of her trach, feeding tube, oxygen feed, and heart monitor.

Many meds were dispensed day and night and Niki's trach tube required suctioning every two hours around the clock. Caring for her was a full-time endeavor. Day by day the Stanleys trusted God to supply the needed grace as their family poured love and care upon frail Niki. In God's kindness, the trach came out much sooner, at her second birthday. Defying the predictions of the doctors, Niki thrived on the love of the Stanley home. By the time she reached high school, she ran track and played soccer. As their second officially adopted daughter, Niki still lives with David and Grace today.

The story goes on with child after child, some staying years, others passing through within months. The Stanleys were chosen to take in a little boy named Sam, one of the first infants diagnosed with pediatric AIDS. (That was back in the early nineties when nobody understood AIDS.) The disease took its toll and Sam died just before his third birthday. Reflecting back on their calling and its challenges, David said, "God places your child into your home for a reason. They are a gift, but they are not really yours; they belong to God. You may not understand all the whys behind their challenges, but it is an opportunity to fully rely on God. When difficulties confronted us, Grace and I didn't have to stop and wonder what to do—you just prayed, did your part, and waited on God." He added, "I still grieve the loss of the children who passed into glory but am comforted by the love of God. I know where they are. I know I will see them again. I'm at peace with that. I just keep coming back to the truth that God's in control. He is doing all things well, and therefore I'm not shaken—I'm not."

Grace became pregnant and gave birth to Kay, who grew up to love and care for her multifaceted family as an extra set of hands God designed to help David and Grace. Lang joined the Stanleys as a malnourished six-month-old when Kay was only three. He was subsequently diagnosed with autism and is the child who led to the phone call that introduced me to Grace and David. One evening Lang announced to Grace, "If you love me, you'll adopt me. You say you love me; do you?" Eight years into his foster care, David and Grace adopted Lang.

Becky and Ginny, twin sisters, were the last two children to join the Stanley clan. Becky was diagnosed with cerebral palsy, and her sister was born seriously frail, needing acute care. Both survived against the odds and were later adopted by the Stanleys. Today, when Becky rides into the church in her motorized wheelchair, she is eager to point out how she and her dad are wearing matching colors. David smiles one of those smiles that lights up a whole room. He and Grace have given up a lot in this life, but have gained so much love. And if we could see the treasure they are storing up in glory—well, let's just say that God will not be outdone.

In addition to his two siblings and their five natural-born children, David and Grace have cared for twenty-five foster children, five of whom they've adopted. Their lives shine as our church looks for the grace we need to follow their example. Their testimony in caring for multiple special-needs children encourages those who are trying to fight for faith to care for one.

David shared, "You know, it says in Hebrews 13 that when you welcome strangers into your home, you never know when you might be entertaining angels. Could the kids we've welcomed into our home be angels, with us unaware? I don't know that they are angels, but our little angels taught us and were sent by God to bless us." Grace added, "As much love as we gave them, they gave us more."

11. What affected you the most about the Stanleys' story?

12. Most folks fear even one of the trials the Stanleys walked through. What can you learn from their trust in God to welcome trial after trial into their home?

Respond

Spend time in group prayer. Pray for one participant's situation, and for other items springing from this week's study.

Before you leave, plan to take one or more of these *action steps* during the coming week.

- Where would you like to see God work evil for good in the life of your children? Formulate these desires into a prayer and offer it up to God.

- Write out your conversion story as a letter to your son or daughter. Tell them in the letter that you want to make sure that they have a record of what God has done in your life. Explain in the concluding paragraphs how God has changed your desires, affections, and dreams. Be sure to include the gospel, but don't use the letter to correct them. Instead, allow the Holy Spirit to use the testimony of your conversion to reach them.

Remember

Memorize Ephesians 2:8–9. "For by grace you have been saved through faith. And this is not your own doing; it is the gift of God, not a result of works, so that no one may boast."

A FINAL THOUGHT

Well, I'm sure this study and my book, *Parenting First Aid*, hasn't solved all your parenting problems or made your trials go away. I'm still dealing with parenting challenges of my own—some larger, some smaller. And on top of those, Lois and I now have two grandchildren with a third on the way. I thought I was getting close to finishing. Our dinner table dropped from eight of us to four. But a new category of trials entered our life when we began watching our grandchildren. Nathan has a baby girl, Charlotte, and Emma has a boy named Zion.

Our ministry as parents continues, and God continues to refine us through the trials he brings, now with grandchildren. But rather than bend under the added weight, our faith is stronger for what we've seen God do. The same God who helped us walk through our own parenting trials is there to help our children walk through theirs. We get to encourage our grown kids and give them a little parenting first aid along the way.